Series/Number 07-111

REGRESSION MODELS
Censored, Sample-Selected, or Truncated Data

RICHARD BREEN
The Queen's University

SAGE PUBLICATIONS
International Educational and Professional Publisher
Thousand Oaks   London   New Delhi

For information address:

SAGE Publications, Inc.
2455 Teller Road
Thousand Oaks, California 91320
E-mail: order@sagepub.com

SAGE Publications Ltd.
6 Bonhill Street
London EC2A 4PU
United Kingdom

SAGE Publications India Pvt. Ltd.
M-32 Market
Greater Kailash I
New Delhi 110 048 India

Printed in the United States of America

Library of Congress Catalog Card No. 89-043409

Breen, Richard, 1954-
    Regression models: Censored, sample-selected, or truncated data /
Richard Breen.
        p.   cm. — (Sage university papers series. Quantitative
applications in the social sciences; v. 111)
    Includes bibliographical references.
    ISBN 0-8039-5710-6 (pbk.: acid-free paper)
    1. Regression analysis.   2. Social sciences—Statistical methods.
I. Title.   II. Series.
QA278.2.B74   1996
300'.01'519536—dc20   95-32527

96 97 98 99 10 9 8 7 6 5 4 3 2 1

Sage Production Editor: Gillian Dickens
Sage Typesetter: Andrea D. Swanson

When citing a university paper, please use the proper form. Remember to cite the current Sage University Paper series title and include the paper number. One of the following formats can be adapted (depending on the style manual used):

(1) BREEN, RICHARD (1996) Regression Models: Censored, Sample-Selected, or Truncated Data. Sage University Paper series on Quantitative Applications in the Social Sciences, 07-111. Thousand Oaks, CA: Sage.

OR

(2) Breen, R. (1996). *Regression models: Censored, sample-selected, or truncated data* (Sage University Paper series on Quantitative Applications in the Social Sciences, series no. 07-111). Thousand Oaks, CA: Sage.

052996/960m

CONTENTS

ACKNOWLEDGMENTS

The author would like to thank Michael Lewis-Beck and a number of anonymous referees for valuable comments on earlier drafts of the manuscript. The book has also benefited greatly from comments and discussions with my colleague, Professor John Spencer.

SERIES EDITOR'S INTRODUCTION

In nonexperimental social science research, regression analysis is the workhorse. After the data are carefully gathered and stored, the analyst almost invariably begins regression runs, applying ordinary least squares (OLS) to the equations he or she has specified. But this OLS impulse, strong as it is, is not always correct. For one, the data may come in certain forms that could render OLS estimates biased. The problematic forms discussed by Professor Breen are censored, sample-selected, or truncated data. Unfortunately, terminology within this literature has much inconsistency. However, examples help clarify things.

Suppose Dr. Barbara Brown, a scholar of urban policy, wants to understand why some U.S. cities spend more than others on air pollution control. She denotes this dependent variable, pollution spending, with a Y. Her independent variables, $X1$ through $X10$, are various overall budget and socioeconomic measures taken on each city. To collect the data, she turns to standard municipal yearbooks. As a first scenario, imagine that in her sample of cities, the amount of annual pollution spending is recorded only when it exceeds $100,000, otherwise the value is missing. That is, Y is *truncated*. However, the X variables are not truncated, instead showing values for all cities. This makes a *censored* sample. If Dr. Brown goes on to apply OLS to her model, what will result? To constitute the data set, she may use only those cases where $Y > \$100,000$. Or, she may assign some value less than $100,000—say $90,000—to those cities that had nothing recorded. In either case, OLS will yield biased estimates.

In the above example, the censoring was caused by the truncation of the dependent variable, Y. A more complex type of censoring occurs when the observation of Y depends on the value of another variable, Z. For this second scenario, let us modify the air pollution illustration slightly. Suppose that everything is the same, but that the municipal yearbooks report air pollution spending only if the city had passed a clean air ordinance. Call this variable Z, scored 1 = passed a clean air ordinance, 0 = otherwise. We now have a *sample selection* problem. Professor Breen's response to the problem is to consider it in two steps: First, what is the probability that a city passed an ordinance? Second, what should the city's spending score be, given that it passed an ordinance? How should the model parameters be estimated? If not by OLS, then Tobit? Heckman two-step? Maximum likelihood? Professor Breen comments on the weaknesses, as well as the strengths, of the different estimation approaches. For instance, in the particular case of censored regression models, he explains how the maximum likelihood Tobit estimator is generally preferred over the Heckman two-stage estimator.

According to Professor Breen, censored, sample-selected, or truncated data pose "pervasive issues in the social sciences." Modern work on these issues began with the seminal paper of James Tobin in 1958. Thus, the series merits a monograph devoted to censored data. Furthermore, it nicely complements our earlier *Event History Analysis* monograph (Allison, No. 46), which deals with another kind of censored data problem.

—*Michael S. Lewis-Beck*
Series Editor

REGRESSION MODELS
Censored, Sample-Selected, or Truncated Data

RICHARD BREEN
The Queen's University of Belfast

1. INTRODUCTION

Consider the following problem. On a school examination, the pass mark is 40%. All students who sit the exam receive a certificate stating whether or not they passed and, if they did, their exam score. A sociologist, researching the factors associated with exam performance, has collected data from a sample of students and wants to assess the effect of explanatory variables, such as social class, gender, and level of parental education, on the students' scores on this exam. But the sociologist's knowledge of the sample members' exam performance comes from the students' own exam certificates. So, if we denote the ith student's exam score by y_i, the sociologist knows the exact score only when $y_i > 39$. Otherwise (for those pupils who failed the exam), he or she knows only that $y_i \leq 39$. The question facing our sociologist is: How do we use the sample data to estimate the relationship that holds between exam score and the explanatory variables in the population? Two naive solutions offer themselves. First, use ordinary least squares (OLS) to regress y on the explanatory variables, using all the observations and assigning all those students who failed a value of $y = 39$.[1] There are several difficulties with this, however, the most significant of which is that the OLS coefficients (that are supposed to tell us how y is related to the explanatory variables) will certainly be biased estimates of their population counterparts (I show why this is so in Chapter 2).

The second solution is to use OLS to regress y on the explanatory variables using only those values for which $y > 39$. But in this case, not only does the discarding of all the observations for which $y \leq 39$ throw away information, but the resulting estimates cannot hold good for the population as a whole because they are based on a nonrandomly selected subset. Once again, the resulting OLS estimates will be biased estimates

1

of the true population parameters. Perhaps more important, and less intuitively obvious, is the fact that *the OLS coefficients are also biased estimates of the parameters among that group of the population for whom* y > *39* (I explain why in Chapter 2).

1.1 Censoring, Sample Selection, and Truncation

The answer to this problem (and the method I develop in the course of this book) is to address it in two steps, or stages. First, we need to examine the probability of an individual passing the exam. In other words, we model the probability that y is greater than 39—which we write as pr $(y > 39)$—conditional on whatever set of variables we believe influences this. Second, we need to model the expected score in the exam conditional on having passed, $E(y|y > 39)$, where E is the expectation operator, conditional on the set of variables we believe influences this. In terms of estimation of the model, these two steps can be undertaken separately or, for greater efficiency, estimated jointly.

The case we have been describing is an example of what, in the statistical literature, is termed a *censored sample problem*. Before specifying exactly what is meant by this, we need to introduce a few terms. A random variable, y, is said to be *truncated from below* (or *left truncated*) if, for some value, c, of y, we know, for all cases where $y > c$, the exact value taken by y, but for all other cases, we only know that $y \leq c$. This is exactly as in the example with which we started. We also could have truncation from above (*right truncation*), where we know the exact values of y in all cases where y is less than some threshold value, c, but for all values equal to or greater than c, we know only that $y \geq c$. A typical example is earnings, where, for the highest earners in a sample, we might know only that their income is, say, \$100,000 per year or more. Finally, we can have multiple truncation with two or more thresholds, such as $d > c$. Here, for $c < y < d$, we observe the exact value of y; for all $y \leq c$, we know only that $y \leq c$, and for all $y \geq d$, we know only that $y \geq d$. This would correspond, for example, to a case in which income was truncated at both high and low values.

Assume now that we have a sample in which y is truncated, but we also have variables, x_k, $k = 1, \ldots K$, of which y is a function. For example, the x_k (or x for short) are the explanatory variables in a regression with y as the dependent variable. Our sample is said to be *censored* if we have observed the values of the x variables for *all* sample observations. So, in the simple case of censoring from below, we would have observed the x values for those cases where $y > c$ (and y is therefore observed exactly), and where y

is only known to be either equal to or less than c. If, on the other hand, we observe the values of the x variables only for those observations where y is recorded exactly, the entire sample is said to be *truncated*. In such a case, we have no information whatsoever on observations whose y value is not observed exactly.

The distinction we have made so far, then, is between a random variable, which may be truncated, and the nature of the complete sample in which the truncated variable is found. The latter can be either a censored sample, if we have some information on the observations whose y values fall in the truncated part of the distribution, or a truncated sample, where we have no such information. In our terminology, we are here following Heckman (1992, p. 205), but this usage is not always followed: Frequently, we see references to censored random variables, for example, and c is described as the "censoring" (rather than the "truncation") threshold. In my view, the terminological niceties are of secondary significance: It is more important that readers understand the difference between censored and truncated samples.

We must then go on to distinguish two broad types of censored samples, depending on the mechanisms that determine whether or not the exact value of the dependent variable, y, is observed. In ordinary censored sample problems, such as the example with which we began, we observe y if it meets some criterion defined in terms of y itself, such as that y must exceed a threshold value, c. But in so-called sample selection problems (Heckman, 1979), whether or not we observe y_i for a given case (in other words, the value of y for the *i*th individual in the sample) depends upon the value of another variable, z_i. A simple example of this is the amount of pocket money (y) given to their children by members of a sample of adults. Because not all adults have children, y could not be observed for this subset of the sample. In this case, $z_i = 1$ if the *i*th sample member has children, $z_i = 0$ otherwise. Here, our two-step approach to the problem would require (a) that we model the probability of adults in our sample having children and (b) that we model the expected value of y, conditional on having children. Therefore, sample selection is a form of censoring, but one in which the truncation of the dependent variable is a function of a second variable. In this case, we would also have two sets of explanatory variables: w, which explains whether or not an adult has children; and x, which explains the observed value of y. We would have complete values of all of the x and w variables for all observations, regardless of whether they were "selected" (in which case we would observe y also) or not (when we would not observe a y value). The x and w variables may have some variables in common, and, indeed, they may be identical. The distinction between what

TABLE 1.1
Censored, Sample-Selected, and Truncated Samples

Sample	y Variable	Explanatory Variables
Censored	y is known exactly only if some criterion defined in terms of the value of y is met, such as $y > c$. y is a truncated random variable.	x variable values are observed for all of the sample, regardless of whether y is known exactly.
Sample selected	y is observed only if some criterion defined in terms of another random variable, z, is met, such as if $z = 1$. y is a truncated random variable.	x and w are observed for all of the sample, regardless of whether y is observed or not.
Truncated	y is observed only if some criterion defined in terms of the value of y is met, such as $y > c$. y is a truncated random variable.	Explanatory variables are observed only if y is observed.

we call censored and sample-selected data is sometimes referred to as one between "explicit" (censoring) and "incidental" (sample selection) selection (Goldberger, 1981).

So now we have three types of sample: censored, sample selected, and truncated. Table 1.1 summarizes the distinctions among them. All three types of problem have a common structure, and, indeed, they are frequently all referred to as problems of censoring. The kinds of statistical models employed to deal with such problems are also sometimes all grouped under the heading of "Tobit models" (Amemiya, 1984), although strictly speaking, the Tobit is only one of several particular models for such data.

1.2 Two-Stage Modeling

The two-stage modeling process we outlined earlier captures the common structure of models of censoring, sample selection, and truncation.[2] In all cases, we have a dependent variable, y, which is completely observed only for a subsample (which we call the selected subsample) of our total sample. Whether y_i is completely observed or not (in other words, whether a given observation falls into the selected subsample) can depend upon the value of y_i itself (in which case we have simple censoring) or upon the value of another variable, z_i (in which case we have a sample selection model). The distinction between censoring and sample selection, on one hand, and truncation, on the other, is that in the former, we have information on both the selected and nonselected subsamples, but in the latter, we have data only on the selected subsample. So, whereas for censored and sample-selected data we can model both the *selection* stage (i.e., the probability that the ith observation is included in the selected sample) and the *outcome* stage (i.e., the expected value of y_i conditional on having been included in the selected sample), for truncated data, we can model only the latter.

One further virtue of adopting this two-stage approach to models of censoring, sample selection, and truncation is that it links the methods introduced in this book with regression models for continuous dependent variables and for the analysis of dichotomous dependent variables (such as logit and probit models). The selection stage essentially involves modeling such a dichotomous dependent variable (selected *versus* not selected), whereas the outcome stage is akin to a regression equation in which a continuous y variable is modeled as a function of a set of explanatory x variables. Thus, this book introduces methods that combine and build upon those described by Lewis-Beck (1980) and Achen (1982) on regression and by Aldrich and Nelson (1984) on methods for the analysis of discrete dependent variables.

Another body of related literature is that dealing with duration data or event history models. In using these models, our interest lies in the length of time that members of a sample spend in one state prior to moving to another (say, from unemployment to a job) and how the risk of making this transition varies across individuals and over time. Usually, our data relate to the observation of the sample over a fixed period of time of length T. Some sample members may not make this transition during this period of time, and thus for them we know only that they spent a period of time at least equal to T in their original state. Such cases are said to be censored. In contrast, for those who made the transition during the study, we know the exact length of time they spent in their original state: These are uncensored observations. Thus, the variable measuring the length of time spent in the original state prior to leaving it is truncated from above at the value T. The parallel with, say, the upper truncation that we might find in a measure of income is very clear, and, indeed, the methods I present in this book could be applied (with some minor modifications) to problems of this kind. In the duration data literature, this approach is known as the accelerated failure time model (Kalbfleisch & Prentice, 1980). Accelerated failure time models are basically censored regression models that express the expected length of time in the original state (or the logarithm of time) as a function of a set of explanatory variables. However, by far the more usual approach to duration data focuses on the "hazard rate" (for a good introduction, see Allison, 1984), although here the distinction between censored and uncensored observations once again plays a crucial role. The analysis of duration data via hazard rate models is now a highly developed area within statistics that we cannot discuss here. However, we will continue to discuss the relationship between censored regression models and accelerated failure time models in Chapter 5.

1.3 Problems of Censoring, Sample Selection, and Truncation in the Social Sciences

Why should we be concerned with censoring, sample selection, and truncation? The simple answer is that they are pervasive issues in the social sciences. The modern literature on the estimation of models for censored data begins with Tobin's (1958) paper, which introduced what was later called the Tobit[3] model. In his paper, Tobin, using data on a sample of 735 households, analyzed the relationship between the ratio of expenditure on durable goods to total disposable income (this was the dependent variable, y), on the one hand, and, on the other, two explanatory variables: the age of the household head and the ratio of liquid assets to total disposable income. In his sample, 183 households had a score of zero on the dependent variable: Thus, y was truncated with a threshold of $c = 0$, and the sample was censored. Since then, the model has been used in many social science disciplines. In political science, for example, Deegan and White (1976) applied it to the analysis of expenditure on TV advertising by candidates for local office in the 1973 Houston city elections: Here, 24 out of the 40 candidates had zero expenditure. In sociology, Walton and Ragin (1990) used the Tobit model to analyze the severity of popular protest in debtor nations. In their sample of 56 countries, 30 had no recorded protests and thus returned a zero score on the dependent variable.

In many cases in which censored regression models might be used, the censoring threshold is zero. Examples include the ownership by households of rarely held goods, such as company shares; expenditure on alcohol; purchases of consumer durables; and so on. There are also cases in which the censoring threshold is nonzero: for example, years of full-time schooling completed (where the threshold would be the legal minimum age for leaving school), and earnings, in those countries that have minimum wage legislation. However, it does not follow that because the dependent variable has an upper or lower (or both) threshold at which at least some observations are clustered, a censored regression model will be the correct choice. We will say more about when the censored regression model is appropriate after we have described the model in detail.

Examples of sample-selected data abound in the social science literature. One area in which sample selection models have been used widely is evaluation research, particularly in the study of the impact of labor market programs, where participation in the program is not a random event. Thus, to analyze the effects of participation (on, say, income or the chances of getting a job) requires that we model both the process of selection into the program and the outcome of the program, conditional on having been selected into it. A good introduction to this approach can be found in Barnow, Cain, and Goldberger (1980).

Research on school effectiveness is another area in which sample selection effects are pervasive (Coleman, Hoffer, & Kilgore, 1982). For example, if we want to look at the relative effects of attending one kind of school rather than another, we need to model both the process by which students are selected into schools of each type and the effects of attending each type of school conditional on having been selected into them.

Item nonresponse in surveys may give rise to sample-selection problems. Suppose, for example, that, in a questionnaire, an item asking respondents about their frequency of sexual intercourse elicits high rates of nonresponse. If the pattern of nonresponse is random, then modeling the factors explaining the frequency of intercourse using OLS regression within the subsample that responded to the item will not cause any problems. However, nonresponse is unlikely to be purely random in this way, and thus, using OLS on only the respondents will yield biased estimates. Again, it would be necessary to adopt a two-stage approach: First, model the process of response/nonresponse; then, model the expected frequency of intercourse, conditional on having responded to the item.

In some cases, sample selection and censoring can co-occur. For example, consider the criminal justice system, and imagine that our interest lies in estimating the effects of determinants of length of custodial sentence given to defendants who plead, or are found, guilty. Here we have a multistage branching process in which, of those who are brought before the courts, only a proportion are found (or plead) guilty; and of this latter group, only a proportion receive a custodial sentence. In the first stage, we might use a sample selection approach to model the process of being found (or pleading) guilty, as opposed to being acquitted. We might then treat the second stage as a case of censoring, so that the same variables that determine whether or not a custodial sentence is given to the guilty also determine the length of sentence. So, we might fit a censored regression model to the sentences received by those found or pleading guilty, but we should also want to correct this for the sample selection bias that might be induced by the necessary omission of those found not guilty. Indeed, the whole criminal justice process might be viewed as comprising not just the two stages outlined, but a whole set of stages (arrest, arraignment, trial, sentencing) that selects ever-smaller subsamples. Ideally, the whole process ought to be modeled as a set of sample selection and censored data problems (Hagan, 1989; Hagan & Parker, 1985; Peterson & Hagan, 1984).

Sampling often can give rise to problems of truncation. For example, researchers often draw a sample taken not from the population as a whole but from that part of the population deemed to be of interest in the study. Therefore, a researcher might survey only those households in the population whose income places them below a poverty line. If, then, the researcher wants to examine the relationship between, say, income and education, the use of OLS regression will almost certainly yield biased coefficient estimates, even if what he or she is interested in is this relationship as it holds for households in poverty (Berk, 1983, p. 388). In this case, we cannot use two-stage methods (designed for censored data) to overcome the problem because, typically, we would have no observations whatsoever on households above the poverty line; thus, we must use techniques for truncated samples. A similar issue arises in studies of the duration of unemployment prior to acquiring a job. Because the unemployed are a nonrandomly selected subset of the whole population, coefficient estimates based on data relating only to the unemployed are likely to be biased.

1.4 Theoretical Basis

In what follows, we assume that the social scientist wants to estimate population parameters regarding the relationship between one or more explanatory or independent variables and a dependent variable. We assume that estimation of these parameters is being carried out on a simple random sample of the population.

The approach taken in this book to the analysis of censored, sample-selected, and truncated data is, as stated earlier, to consider the problem as comprising two stages and model each of these. The reason for adopting this approach is easy to explain. By a standard statistical result, we can write the expected value of a random variable, v, as the sum of the products of the probability of v falling into one of a set of disjoint intervals, and the expected value of v in that interval. We let I_m ($m = 1, 2, \ldots$ M) denote the intervals

$$E(v) = \sum_{m=1}^{M} \text{pr}(v \in I_m)E(v \mid v \in I_m). \tag{1.1}$$

Here, $\text{pr}(v \in I_m)$ means the probability that a value of v falls in the mth interval. Therefore, the expected value of a random variable can be expressed as the sum of its conditional expectations, $(E[v \mid v \in I_m])$, multiplied by their probability $(\text{pr}[v \in I_m])$. The result shown in Equation 1.1 is a simplified version of what is sometimes called the "law of total probability for expectations" (Karlin & Taylor, 1975, p. 8).

Applying this to the problem of censoring, consider the normal regression in which we have

$$E(y_i|x_i) = x_i'\beta, \tag{1.2}$$

where the subscript i denotes the ith individual in the sample, and both x and β are column vectors.

If we consider a dichotomizing of the values of y around a constant c, then, using the result shown in Equation 1.1, we can rewrite the left-hand side of Equation 1.2 as follows:

$$E(y_i|x_i) = \text{pr}(y_i > c \mid x_i)E(y_i| y_i > c, x_i) \tag{1.3}$$
$$+ \text{pr}(y_i \leq c \mid x_i)E(y_i|y_i \leq c, x_i).$$

In this case, the intervals referred to in Equation 1.1 are defined on the variable y itself: I_1 is defined as the interval $(-\infty, c]$ and I_2 is the interval $(c, +\infty)$. Here, the probability that y exceeds or does not exceed c is written as depending upon x, whereas the expectation parts of the equation are conditional upon both x and whether y is greater than or less than c. Because y is dichotomized with respect to c, the probability that y is less than or equal to c is equal to one minus the probability that y is greater than c. Therefore, we can write Equation 1.3 as:

$$E(y_i|x_i) = \text{pr}(y_i > c \mid x_i)E(y_i| y_i > c, x_i) \tag{1.4}$$
$$+ [1 - \text{pr}(y_i > c \mid x_i)]E(y_i|y_i \leq c, x_i).$$

If we have truncation of y from below at the value c, then the expected value of our observed variable is simply

$$E(y_i \,|x_i) = \text{pr}(y_i > c\, |\, x_i)E(y_i|\, y_i > c, \, x_i) \tag{1.5}$$
$$+ \, [1 - \text{pr}(y_i > c|\, x_i)] \times c.$$

Note that the final conditional expectation has been replaced in Equation 1.5 by the constant, c. This is wholly innocuous because we can always set $c = 0$ by defining $z = y - c$ and taking z as our dependent variable. This will have the effect of changing the original estimate of the intercept, α, to an estimate of $\alpha - c$, but it will leave the estimates of the slope coefficients unchanged. It now follows that we need to estimate only the two parts of the equation that we discussed earlier, namely the selection step (i.e., in this case, the probability of an observation not being censored) and the outcome step (the expected value of the observation conditional on not being censored). Both of these are assumed to be functions of the same set of variables, x.

In fact, the model is not as restrictive as this might imply. The selection and outcome processes do not have to be functions of the same set of variables. To refer again to Equation 1.1, the intervals need not be defined with respect to the random variable, v. Rather, they might be defined with respect to another variable, say, z. Likewise, the process of selection might be more complicated than this example suggests. We have already mentioned the case of doubly truncated (with upper and lower limits) data, but we might also have complicated sample selection, so that, for example, y is only observed if two criteria are met. That is, we might observe y_i only if, for two random variables, z and r, both $z_i > 0$ and $r_i > 0$. In such a case, the model would be:

$$E(y_i) = \text{pr}(z_i > 0, \, r_i > 0)E(y_i|\, z_i > 0, \, r_i > 0).$$

Here, for ease of notation, we have omitted the dependence of both parts of the model on independent variables, but we might well have a case in which r, y, and z were all modeled as functions of different sets of explanatory variables. Furthermore, if r and z were not independent, then modeling the process of selection would require the modeling of a bivariate probability distribution.

A more fundamental complication arises if the two stages are considered to be simultaneous rather than sequential. For example, suppose we are interested in the factors associated with how much people earn. In a random sample of working-age adults, not all will have a job, and thus the dependent variable, earnings (or some suitable transformation of earnings), will be observed only for some members of the sample. If we further assume that people take a job only if it pays above the minimum level they consider acceptable—their "reservation wage," as it is sometimes known—then the selection stage (does the individual have a job?) and the outcome stage (what is the person's wage, given that he or she has a job?) are not sequential. Rather, they are simultaneous. A person will be observed to have a job only if the job pays more than that person's reservation wage. We will discuss this model in Chapter 5. Although such simultaneity complicates estimation of the model, we believe that it still remains useful to conceptualize the problem using the two-stage framework.

1.5 Contents of the Book

In the next chapter, we begin with the simplest example of estimation involving a censored sample, Tobin's (1958) Tobit model. We spend a good deal of time discussing this model, dealing with issues such as maximum likelihood estimation and the interpretation of parameters, which we draw on in subsequent chapters. We then go on in Chapter 3 to discuss the basic sample-selection model and the truncated regression model. Chapter 4 elaborates on the modeling of censored and sample-selected data via maximum likelihood, showing the close links between the models introduced in this monograph and other regression models for noncontinuous dependent variables, such as the ordered probit. We also show how the approach can be extended to cases in which the selection and outcome step cannot be modeled as sequential.

Chapter 5 examines some of the criticisms that have been made of these approaches and the difficulties associated with them, and it seeks to give some guide to the practical utility of these models as well as pointing readers toward some alternatives.

Notes

1. We assume that although y has an upper bound, this can be ignored for purposes of estimation.
2. This common structure was first pointed out by Heckman (1976), who, drawing on earlier work by Gronau (1974) and Lewis (1974), developed the two-step approach to the problem that we use in this book.
3. Tobit is short for "Tobin's probit."

2. THE TOBIT MODEL FOR CENSORED DATA

The simplest model for censored data is the so-called Tobit model, from Tobin (1958). The issue with which the Tobit model deals is of the kind discussed in the introduction to the previous chapter. Here, we motivate the discussion using a different example based on Tobin's (1958) original application of the model. Let y_i be the monthly expenditure on luxury goods of the ith household in a random sample of households, and let x_i be a vector of values of explanatory variables (such as monthly income, wealth, measures of family composition, and so forth) for the corresponding household. We want to estimate the vector β, which contains the set of population regression parameters relating the variables that make up x_i to expenditure on luxury goods. Our sample comprises N households, of which N_0 spend nothing on luxury goods and N_1 $(= N - N_0)$ spend something.

2.1 Censored Latent Variables

One very common interpretation of the Tobit and other, similar models is in terms of an underlying latent variable, y^*, of which y is the realized observation. In the case of our earlier example of exam performance, the latent variable was the individual student's actual exam score (varying from 0 to 100), but this was observed only if a threshold value was exceeded. So the true exam score would be denoted y^* and the observed result (the score truncated at 39) would be denoted y. Likewise, in the present example, y^* might be the propensity or capacity of households to spend income on luxury goods, but this is only realized as actual expenditure, y, if that capacity exceeds zero. So, although many observations may have an identical score of zero on the realized variable, they can be considered as having differing scores on the latent variable. The model can be written in terms of the underlying or latent variable as:

$$y_i^* = x_i'\beta + u_i \qquad (2.1)$$

and we assume that the u_i are independent and normally distributed errors with a zero mean and constant variance, σ^2. It is important to be aware that we are also assuming that Equation 2.1 is the correct functional form for the relationship between the latent variable and the x variables, that the x variables have been measured without error, and that we have not omitted any relevant x variables from the specification. None of these assumptions is trivial, and before using the Tobit, we need to consider whether or not our data conform to them. The consequences of violating these assumptions are well known for OLS regression, but they are less well known for the Tobit and the other models discussed in this monograph. However (and as we discuss more fully in Chapter 5), it is known that these models are less robust to the violation of certain assumptions (such as the assumption of normality) than are OLS models. This does not mean that these models are too fragile to use: Clearly, if OLS is known to be inappropriate (as in the examples discussed here), it is not sensible to persist with it in the hope that it may turn out to be more robust to other actual or suspected problems. Rather, it is important to try to check that our assumptions hold, to transform data to fit the assumptions where possible, and to design and undertake research so as to minimize such problems.

The relationship between the observed and latent variables can be written simply as:

$$y_i = y_i^* \text{ if } y_i^* > c;$$

$$y_i = c \text{ if } y_i^* \leq c,$$

where c is the threshold for censoring ($c = 0$ in the examples we have been discussing).

Our model, written in terms of the observed variable, y, and letting $c = 0$, is therefore:

$$y_i = x_i'\beta + u_i \text{ if } y_i > 0$$

$$y_i = 0 \text{ otherwise.}$$

Equation 1.5 of Chapter 1 showed the formula for the expected value of a variable (conditional on x_i) censored at c. In this case, because $c = 0$, it reduces to

$$E(y_i \mid x_i) = \text{pr}(y_i > 0 \mid x_i)E(y_i \mid y_i > 0, x_i). \tag{2.2}$$

We now show how to estimate such a model using our two-stage approach.

14

2.2 Two-Stage Modeling

2.2.1 Selection

To begin with, note that $y_i > 0$ implies

$$x_i'\beta + u_i > 0$$

and thus

$$u_i > -x_i'\beta. \tag{2.3}$$

In other words, the probability that $y_i > 0$ is simply equal to the probability that u_i exceeds $-x_i'\beta$. But because u_i has a normal distribution, this is the same as asking, What is the probability that a normally distributed random variable exceeds this value? If we recall the procedure for carrying out z tests, we remember that a table of areas under the standard normal curve tells us the probability that a normally distributed random variable, standardized to have a mean of zero and standard deviation of 1, is *less than or equal to* that value of z. Our case, however, is slightly different, in that we want to know the probability that u_i *exceeds* z_i^*, where $z_i^* = -x_i'\beta$. However, because the normal distribution is symmetric, the probability that a normally distributed random variable exceeds z is equal to the probability that it is less than $-z$. So, in our case,

$$\text{pr}(u_i > -x_i'\beta) = \text{pr}(u_i \leq x_i'\beta).$$

The probability that a normally distributed random variable with a zero mean and a variance of σ^2 is less than or equal to $x_i'\beta$ is denoted $F(x_i'\beta, \sigma^2)$, or F_i for short. This is

$$F_i = F(x_i'\beta, \sigma^2) = \int_{-\infty}^{x_i'\beta} \frac{1}{\sqrt{2\pi\sigma^2}} \exp(-t^2/2\sigma^2)dt.$$

This probability is equal to the proportion of the area under a normal curve with a mean of zero and a standard deviation of σ that lies between $-\infty$ and

$\mathbf{x}_i'\beta$. In turn, however, F_i is equal to a quantity we denote $\Phi(\mathbf{x}_i'\beta/\sigma)$, or Φ_i for short, where

$$\Phi_i \equiv \Phi\left(\frac{x_i'\beta}{\sigma}\right) = \int_{-\infty}^{x_i'\beta/\sigma} \frac{1}{\sqrt{2\pi}} \exp(-t^2/2)dt. \tag{2.4}$$

Equation 2.4 is called the standard normal distribution function, and it tells us the probability that a *standardized* normally distributed random variable (with mean zero and standard deviation of one) is less than or equal to $\mathbf{x}_i'\beta/\sigma$. This probability is equal to the proportion of the area under the standard normal curve that lies between $-\infty$ and $\mathbf{x}_i'\beta/\sigma$.

This probability—whether we denote it F_i or Φ_i (and we shall use the latter)—can be estimated using a probit model (Aldrich & Nelson, 1984, pp. 48-49). In the probit model, σ and β are not separately identified. The parameter estimates for this model are thus β/σ, but it is usually assumed, for convenience, that $\sigma = 1$ (e.g., see Maddala, 1983, p. 23).

2.2.2 Outcome

Note that if Condition 2.3 is not met, we have a zero observation on y_i. Hence, we need to estimate only the expected value of y, conditional on $y > 0$. We can write this as

$$E(y_i \mid y_i > 0, x_i) = x_i'\beta + E(u_i \mid u_i > -x_i'\beta). \tag{2.5a}$$

Recall that y will exceed zero only when this condition on u is met. So, instead of having the expression $E(u_i)$ in the model (as in a normal OLS), we have the conditional expectation $E(u_i \mid u_i > -x_i'\beta)$. Because we have already assumed that the unconditional expectation of u is zero, the conditional expectation will be nonzero. Hence, we have what is, in effect, an extra term in our regression equation. Our problem, then, is how to model this extra term. To do this, we need a result from statistical theory that will tell us the expected value of a truncated, normally distributed random variable. The results that we use are given in Appendix A. Recall that u is a normally distributed random variable, in this case truncated from below at $-x_i'\beta$. Using the required standard result for the expectation of a truncated, normal random variable, we can write

$$E(u_i \mid u_i > -x_i'\beta) = \sigma \frac{\phi_i}{\Phi_i} . \qquad (2.5b)$$

Here, Φ_i is, once again, the standard normal distribution function evaluated at $x_i'\beta/\sigma$. ϕ_i is the corresponding standard normal density function evaluated at the same point; that is,

$$\phi_i \equiv \phi\left(\frac{x_i'\beta}{\sigma}\right) = \frac{1}{\sqrt{2\pi}} \exp\frac{(-x_i'\beta)^2}{2\sigma^2} .$$

It is important to distinguish between Φ_i, which is a probability, and ϕ_i, which is the density that corresponds to that probability. The ratio of the density to the distribution function (ϕ_i/Φ_i), which appears in Equation 2.5b, is known as the "inverse Mill's ratio," or the hazard rate, and is usually symbolized by λ_i. Thus, we can write

$$x_i'\beta + E(u_i \mid u_i > -x_i'\beta) = x_i'\beta + \sigma \frac{\phi_i}{\Phi_i} \qquad (2.6)$$

$$= x_i'\beta + \sigma\lambda_i.$$

This equation can be estimated very easily. From the results of our selection stage probit model, we can obtain fitted values in the form of estimated probabilities that a given observation has a y value exceeding zero: These are estimates of Φ. We can also obtain estimates of the corresponding ϕ (given by the standard normal density evaluated at $(x_i'\beta)/\sigma$ for the ith observation). For those observations that have y_i values greater than zero, we use these estimates of Φ_i and ϕ_i to calculate estimates of λ_i, the inverse Mill's ratio. We then use OLS to regress the nonzero y values on the x_i and the estimated λ to obtain estimates of β and σ:

$$E(y_i \mid y_i > 0, x_i) = x_i'\beta + \sigma\hat{\lambda}_i. \qquad (2.7)$$

Another way to estimate the model is to use Equation 2.2, which expresses the expected value of y_i as the product of the probability that $y_i > 0$ and the expected value of y_i, conditional on $y_i > 0$. We write this as

$$E(y_i \mid x_i) = \Phi_i\left[x_i'\beta + \sigma\,\frac{\varphi_i}{\Phi_i}\right]. \tag{2.8}$$

To estimate this equation, we take the results of the probit, which give us the first part of this—namely Φ_i. The conditional expectation of y is then given by Equation 2.5a. So, replacing Φ_i and ϕ_i with their estimated values (from the probit), we can then cancel in Equation 2.8 to obtain

$$E(y_i \mid x_i) = \hat{\Phi}_i\beta x_i + \sigma\hat{\phi}_i. \tag{2.9}$$

This can once again be estimated by OLS, but this time using all of the sample observations.

This estimator of β (derived from either Equation 2.7 or 2.9) is sometimes known as the Heckman two-step estimator (Amemiya, 1984), following Heckman (1976, 1979). Although this approach is very straightforward and easy to apply, there are some difficulties with it—notably, that the estimated standard errors of the coefficients and the estimate of σ are all incorrect. We discuss this further when we look at an example.

2.3 Maximum Likelihood Estimation

A method of estimation of the Tobit model that overcomes these difficulties is maximum likelihood (ML). Unfortunately, ML is likely to be less familiar to readers than the more usual OLS techniques. Nevertheless, it is a sufficiently important and widely used method of estimation in all areas of statistics and econometrics (including the analysis of censored, sample-selected, and truncated data) to make it worth our while spending a little time explaining the basics of it (see also Aldrich & Nelson, 1984, chap. 3; Eliason, 1993; Kmenta, 1971, pp. 174-182).

Consider first a regression model with one dependent (y) and one independent (x) variable. The output of the regression package we use will give us estimates of three basic parameters: These are α, the intercept; β, the regression coefficient; and σ, the standard error of the assumed normally distributed, independent error term. Estimates of α and β usually will be obtained by the method of least squares, and, if various conditions (homoscedasticity, serial independence of the u_i, zero expectation of the u_i, and zero correlation between u and x) are met, then the OLS estimator of α and β will be the best linear unbiased estimator (BLUE) (e.g., see Johnston, 1972, chaps. 2 and 5). This simply means that the least squares estimator will be the most efficient (i.e., have the smallest sampling variance) of all linear, unbiased estimators.

However, there is another way to estimate α, β, and σ, and this is to use ML. The basic idea of ML is to find that set of estimates of the parameters that, if these parameter estimates were true of the population, would have most likely generated the observed sample data (or, more strictly, that would have generated the observed sample most often). For a set of N sample observations, y_1, y_2, ... y_N, on the random variable y, we ask: What is the likelihood of having drawn these particular observations from our population, given a certain set of population parameter values? In ML estimation, we "try out" different possible values of these population parameters until we find the set that maximizes this likelihood. It follows, then, that to carry out ML estimation, we need to be able to write down an expression for the likelihood of observing the particular pattern of y_i values in our sample.

A straightforward distribution that we can use to illustrate how this is done is the binomial, which, as we will demonstrate, can give rise to the widely used probit model. A binomially distributed random variable takes only two possible values, which we call 0 and 1, and the distribution itself is characterized by only one parameter, its mean, which we write as π. This is equal to the probability of the variable giving rise to a value of 1. Hence, the probability of getting a value of 0 is simply $1 - \pi$. The probability distribution of a binomially distributed random variable, y, is thus

$$f(y) = \pi^y (1 - \pi)^{1 - y}.$$

This is the expression for the probability of observing a particular value (either 0 or 1) of the random variable. If we draw a sample of N values from this distribution, we can write its joint probability distribution as

$$f(y_1, y_2 \ldots y_N).$$

This is the expression for the probability of having drawn the particular pattern of 0s and 1s in our sample of size N. If our sample observations are independent, this joint probability reduces to the product of the marginal probabilities:

$$f(y_1)f(y_2) \ldots f(y_N).$$

Substituting the particular form for f, we get

$$\pi^{y_1}(1-\pi)^{1-y_1}\pi^{y_2}(1-\pi)^{1-y_2}\ldots\pi^{y_N}(1-\pi)^{1-y_N} \qquad (2.10)$$

$$= \prod_1^N \pi^{y_i}(1-\pi)^{1-y_i}.$$

This latter expression is called the likelihood function. But why is it called the likelihood when it appears identical to the joint probability distribution of the sample? The answer is that, although the two are indeed identically written, whereas the joint probability distribution takes the parameters of the distribution (in this case, π) to be fixed and the specific y values to be variable, in the likelihood, the situation is reversed. Here, the values are fixed (they are the observed values of y in our sample), and the parameters are allowed to vary. Indeed, once we have written down the likelihood function, our next step entails finding those parameters that, given the values of our sample observations, maximize this function. In practice, it is usually easier to work with the natural logarithm of the likelihood function, called the log-likelihood, which we denote L. Because the logarithm of the likelihood is a monotonic transformation of the likelihood, both functions have their maximum at the same point. In this example, the log-likelihood is

$$L = \sum_{i=1}^N [y_i \log\pi + (1-y_i)\log(1-\pi)]. \qquad (2.11)$$

Suppose that our sample comprises 2,000 observations of y, of which 1,472 take the value 1 and the remaining 528 the value 0. To estimate the unknown parameter π (which must lie between 0 and 1), we would substitute possible values into Equation 2.11. If our first guess was $\pi = 0.5$, we would get a value for the log-likelihood function of

$$L = 1{,}472 \times \log(0.5) + 528 \times \log(1-0.5) = -1386.29.$$

Table 2.1 shows the values of L for various "guesses" of the value of π. The function is maximized at the value 0.7. In fact, a finer search would show that a value of 0.736 maximizes the log-likelihood, and this would be our maximum likelihood (ML) estimate of the parameter π.

Simply estimating π, however, is not a particularly interesting use of maximum likelihood. Indeed, the maximum likelihood estimator of π is

TABLE 2.1
Values of the Log-Likelihood Function for Different Estimates of π

Estimate of π	Log-Likelihood Function
0.1	−3445.04
0.2	−2486.91
0.3	−1960.57
0.4	−1618.50
0.5	−1386.29
0.6	−1235.74
0.7	−1160.72
0.8	−1178.25
0.9	−1370.86

simply the proportion of 1s that we observe in our sample data. However, we can make π a function of data and parameters. Suppose that for each y_i in our sample, we have a corresponding measure x_i, which we assume is a continuous variable. We could write $\pi_i = f(x_i)$, where f is some function. In probit analysis, we have

$$\pi_i = \Phi(\alpha + \gamma x_i),$$

where, once again, Φ denotes the standard normal distribution function, and we assume $\sigma = 1$.

Substituting this expression in Equation 2.11, we get the log-likelihood:

$$L = \sum_{i=1}^{N} [y_i \log(\Phi_i) + (1 - y_i) \log(1 - \Phi_i)] \tag{2.12}$$

$$\text{where } \Phi_i \equiv \Phi(\alpha + \gamma x_i) .$$

This is the expression for the log-likelihood of the probit model (Aldrich & Nelson, 1984, p. 51). By maximizing this with respect to the parameters α and γ, we get the ML estimates of these parameters. Of course, in this case, the naive method we used to search for our ML estimate of π will not be adequate, and more complex approaches to maximizing the log-likelihood are needed (see Eliason, 1993, chap. 3).

As a second example, suppose that y, rather than being a categorical or discrete variable, is continuous. Exactly the same general procedure for

ML estimation would be followed. Once again, we seek the set of population parameters that maximizes the likelihood function, and to write down the likelihood function we need to know the joint probability distribution of our sample data. The major difference from the example we presented above comes at this point: whereas, in the case of a categorical or discrete variable, we can write down the probability of its taking a specific value (in other words, such a random variable has a well-defined probability mass function), this is not true of continuous variables. So, in the case when y was dichotomous, it made sense to speak of the probability that y took the value 0 or 1; but for a continuous variable, we cannot speak of the probability that it takes a particular value. Therefore, we cannot use the probability mass function in the likelihood. Rather, we use the density function, which, loosely speaking, fulfills the same role in expressions involving continuous variables as does the probability mass function in expressions involving discrete variables.[1]

If we assume that the y_i's in the population are distributed normally around their mean, we can write the density function as

$$f(y_i) = \frac{1}{\sqrt{2\pi\sigma^2}} \exp \frac{-[(y_i - \mu)/\sigma]^2}{2} .$$

The likelihood function is thus the product of these densities over all the y_i's. Taking logarithms gives the following log-likelihood function:

$$L = \sum_{1}^{N} \log\left(\frac{1}{\sqrt{2\pi\sigma^2}}\right) - \frac{1}{2\sigma^2}(y_i - \mu)^2 . \tag{2.13a}$$

Once again, maximizing this function will give us estimates of μ and σ. If we assume that μ varies over our sample members, write $\mu_i = \alpha + \beta x_i$, and insert this in the log-likelihood, we get the log-likelihood for an OLS regression of y on x:

$$L = \sum_{1}^{N} \log\left(\frac{1}{\sqrt{2\pi\sigma^2}}\right) - \frac{1}{2\sigma^2}[y_i - (\alpha + \beta x_i)]^2 . \tag{2.13b}$$

Maximizing this expression with respect to α, β, and σ will give us the maximum likelihood estimates (MLEs) of these parameters.

ML estimators have a number of desirable properties. However, these are known to hold only when the sample size is large (and when certain relatively mild regularity conditions also hold). In statistical terms, ML estimators have desirable asymptotic properties. These are slightly different from those of OLS estimators (which hold, of course, when the conditions for OLS—homoscedasticity, independence of errors, zero expectation of errors, and zero correlation between explanatory variables and the error term—are met). So, OLS estimates are unbiased, which means that the expected value of a parameter estimated by OLS is equal to the true population value of that parameter,

$$E(\hat{\theta}) = \theta,$$

where $\hat{\theta}$ is the OLS estimate of the parameter. ML estimates, however, are consistent rather than unbiased. This means that the distribution of the ML estimator becomes more concentrated around the true value of the parameter as the sample size increases (Kmenta, 1971, pp. 133-134, 181-182). This is not the same as saying that the estimator is asymptotically unbiased—which means that, in the limit, as the sample size grows very large, the expected value of the estimate of the parameter comes to equal its true value.[2] ML estimates are always consistent, but they can be asymptotically biased. However, as Eliason (1993, p. 20) notes, for all practical purposes, and for all the models discussed in this monograph, the maximum likelihood estimators, in fact, also will be asymptotically unbiased.

OLS estimators are efficient, which simply means that the variance of a parameter estimated using OLS is smaller than the variance of the same parameter estimated by any other linear, unbiased estimator. ML estimators, however, are asymptotically efficient; that is, once again they have the property of efficiency only when the sample size is large. Finally, if we assume that the error term is normally distributed in the population, it follows that the estimated OLS coefficients have a normal distribution also, and thus we can calculate confidence intervals around them and employ standard statistical tests of significance. ML estimates are said to be asymptotically normally distributed, which once again means that the ML estimates of a parameter are normally distributed for large samples but not necessarily for small ones. The variances of ML parameters are obtained very easily as the diagonal elements of the inverse of what is termed the "information matrix." The information matrix is the negative of the expected values of the matrix of second partial derivatives of the log-likelihood function with respect to the parameters (see Aldrich & Nelson, 1984, p. 54; Eliason, 1994, p. 20; Kmenta, 1971, p. 182). However, these are asymptotic variances of the parameters, applicable only when the sample size is large.

ML is a very general and flexible technique: If we can write down the likelihood function—which in turn depends on assumptions about how the sample data have been generated—we can, in principle, estimate the population parameters. In practice, however, we must pay attention to how well behaved the log-likelihood function is.[3] One important question is whether or not it possesses a single maximum. If, for example, the function possesses several local maxima, the parameter estimates may depend on the starting values from which the estimation begins. The Tobit log-likelihood does not have this problem because it is known to have a single maximum; that is, it is a globally concave function (Olsen, 1978).

2.4 Maximum Likelihood Estimation of the Tobit Model

To write down the likelihood function for the Tobit model, consider what we know about our sample and what assumptions we are making. For concreteness, we use the example of expenditure on luxury goods that we introduced at the start of this chapter. First, we assume that u_i has a normal distribution, that errors for different observations are independent, and that the error term is independent of the explanatory variables in the model. Second, for all the sample households, we know whether or not they spent something on luxury goods. Third, for the N_1 noncensored observations, we know how much they spent. We use these three pieces of information to form the likelihood function for all observations. So, for all observations, we know whether or not they were censored; thus, the censored observations contribute the following term to the likelihood

$$\prod_0 (1 - \Phi_i). \tag{2.14a}$$

That is, the likelihood contains the product, taken over all N_0 observations that were censored, of the probability that they were censored (equal to one minus the probability that they were uncensored).

The uncensored observations contribute the following term:

$$\prod_1 \Phi_i \ . \tag{2.14b}$$

The likelihood thus contains the product, taken over all N_1 uncensored observations, of the probability that they were uncensored. Finally, for the uncensored observations, we know the amount of their expenditure; hence, they also contribute the following term to the likelihood:

$$\prod_1 \frac{1}{\sigma} \frac{\phi[(y_i - x_i'\beta)/\sigma]}{\Phi_i} \ . \tag{2.14c}$$

This is the density function for a truncated normal distribution. Because Φ_i appears in the numerator of Equation 2.14b and the denominator of Equation 2.14c (both of which apply to the uncensored observations), these cancel. Putting the result together with Equation 2.14a, the likelihood function is

$$l = \prod_0 [1 - \Phi_i] \prod_1 \phi[(y_i - x_i'\beta)/\sigma].$$

For estimation, we use the logarithm of the likelihood function, which, in this case, can be written

$$L = \sum_0 \log(1 - \Phi_i) + \sum_1 \log\frac{1}{\sqrt{2\pi\sigma^2}} - \sum_1 \frac{1}{2\sigma^2}(y_i - x_i'\beta)^2 \ . \tag{2.15}$$

This is the complete log-likelihood for the Tobit model. Note that the part of the log-likelihood that is summed over the uncensored observations is exactly the same as the log-likelihood for the normal error regression model given in Equation 2.13b.

To illustrate the methods we have been discussing, we use some simulated data. We begin with a population in which

$$y_i^* = 1 + 2x_i + u_i,$$

where u_i is normally distributed with a mean of zero and standard deviation of 2. Thus, in the population, we have $\beta = 2$ and also $\sigma = 2$. We then draw a sample of 2,000 observations from this population. Our goal is to use these sample data to estimate β and σ. Given that these are simulated data, we can begin by simply regressing the latent variable y^* on x in the sample. If we do this, we get an estimate of $\beta = 2.126$ (standard error = .052); α (the intercept term) = .927 (.053); and $\sigma = 2.02$.

If we now censor the sample at zero, we can define the variable y as

$$y_i = y^*_i \text{ if } y^*_i > 0$$

$$y_i = 0 \text{ if } y^*_i \leq 0.$$

In our sample, this gives us 472 zero observations on y. To estimate β and σ, we can try four methods as follows:

A. OLS regression of y on x using all observations
B. OLS regression of y on x using only the nonzero y observations
C. The Heckman two-step estimator
D. The ML Tobit

The results of fitting these four models are shown in Table 2.2. These yield somewhat different estimates of both β and σ, as can be seen. What is immediately striking, however, is the very close agreement between the Tobit results and the OLS results when we regress y^* on x (of course, if these were real data, we would not have observations on y^* and so would be unable to make this comparison). The Heckman parameters also come very close to these values. In contrast, the OLS estimates using y or the values of y that are greater than zero are very far away from the population values for both β and σ. This is because these estimates are biased, as we pointed out in Chapter 1. In the case of Method A, using all the observations on y, the source of bias is easy to see. Equations 2.8 and 2.9 give us the correct model for the unconditional expected value of the ys: Regressing the y values on x cannot give us an estimate of the regression coefficient that will equal that derived from Equation 2.9 except in the special case of $\Phi_i = 1$ for all i (and thus $\phi_i = 0$ in all cases). But Φ_i is the probability that the ith observation is uncensored, and because at least some observations are censored, there must be at least some cases for which this is not equal to unity. Thus, if the coefficients from Equation 2.9 are unbiased, it follows that the coefficients from Method A must be biased.

TABLE 2.2
Estimation Results for Simulated Censored Data
(standard errors in parentheses)

Method	Estimates of		
	α	β	σ
(A) OLS (using all observations on y	1.529	1.681	1.676
including $y_i = 0$)	(0.043)	(0.043)	
(B) OLS ($y_i > 0$ only)	2.085	1.386	1.704
	(0.060)	(0.054)	
(C) Heckman 2-step			
Probit	0.466	1.084	1.000
	(0.010)	(0.010)	
Regression	0.846	2.174	2.178
	(0.266)	(0.174)	(0.456)
(D) Tobit	0.929	2.125	2.022
	(0.059)	(0.056)	(0.038)

Regression of y^* on x: $E(y^*_i) = 0.927 + 2.126x_i$
$\qquad\qquad\qquad\qquad$ (.053) (.052)

In the case of Method B, which uses only the strictly positive y values, we know that $E(y|y > 0)$ is given by Equation 2.7. This equation cannot be estimated by regressing the positive ys on x because it contradicts two of the central assumptions that ensure the unbiasedness and consistency of OLS—namely, that u has a mean of zero and that u and x are uncorrelated. In this case, $E(u_i|u_i > -\beta x_i)$ cannot equal zero (because the unconditional expectation of u equals zero) and will, in fact, be a function of x_i (Maddala, 1983, p. 2). Hence, the coefficients of Method B are biased estimates of the population β. In other words, as we pointed out in Chapter 1, using OLS on the noncensored observations will not yield unbiased parameter estimates even for the noncensored part of the population.

Concentrating now on Methods C and D in Table 2.2, we note that, in the Heckman probit equation, the estimate of σ is set to unity, as mentioned earlier. Recall, however, that both the probit and the Tobit coefficients can be used to calculate Φ_i; therefore, we would like them to agree. In both cases, the probabilities are evaluated at $\beta x_i/\sigma$. This implies that the Tobit coefficients should be roughly 2.022 times as large as those from the probit. As Table 2.2 shows, this relationship holds approximately: The Tobit coefficients are just less than twice their probit counterparts.

Finally, we stated earlier that σ and the standard errors are incorrectly estimated when we use OLS in the second equation of the Heckman method. The Heckman method gives consistent estimates of β but not of σ, nor are the asymptotic standard errors consistent. As a result, adjustments must be made to the regression results. These adjustments are relatively straightforward, as we show in Chapter 3. In the case of censored regression models, however, there is nothing to be gained from using the Heckman two-step estimator rather than the ML Tobit estimator, particularly now that the latter is readily available in many computer programs. However, the two-step method has been used widely in much of what we deal with in later chapters.

2.5 Interpretation of Tobit Parameters

In interpreting the results of a Tobit, we can examine the estimated parameters with reference to four kinds of expected value. These are

(a) the expected value of the underlying latent variable. In the Tobit model, this is

$$E(y^*_i \mid x_i) = x_i'\beta \qquad (2.16)$$

(b) the estimated probability of exceeding the censoring threshold, c:

$$\text{pr}(y_i > c) = \Phi\left(\frac{x_i'\beta}{\sigma}\right) \qquad (2.17)$$

(c) the expected, unconditional value of the realized variable:

$$E(y_i \mid x_i) = \Phi_i\left(x_i'\beta + \sigma\,\frac{\phi_i}{\Phi_i}\right) + (1 - \Phi_i)c \qquad (2.18)$$

(d) the expected value of the realized variable, conditional on this being greater than the threshold value, c:

$$E(y_i \mid y > c, x_i) = x_i'\beta + \sigma\frac{\phi_i}{\Phi_i} + c \qquad (2.19)$$

It is important to be aware of the differences among these four expected values. The Tobit coefficients that are typically produced by Tobit ML estimation routines in packages such as LIMDEP and SHAZAM (among others) relate directly to the unobserved latent variable, y^*. Thus, taken by themselves, each shows the effect of a change in a given x variable on the expected value of the latent variable, holding all other x variables constant. In other words, with respect to the latent variable, Tobit βs can be interpreted in just the same way as the βs from an OLS.

The coefficients, therefore, cannot be given the same interpretation when we turn to (b), (c), or (d). Here, the effect of a unit change in one of the x variables on the dependent variable is not straightforwardly given by the relevant β coefficient, because if a given x variable changes, so too do the values of ϕ and Φ, one or both of which enter into the expressions for the expected value of $pr(y > c)$ and for $E(y)$ and $E(y \mid y > c)$. Thus, the partial derivatives are slightly more difficult to compute. The full set for (a) through (d) is as follows:

$$\frac{\partial E(y^*)}{\partial x_j} = \beta_j \tag{2.20a}$$

$$\frac{\partial pr(y > 0)}{\partial x_j} = \phi(z)\frac{\beta_j}{\sigma} \tag{2.20b}$$

$$\frac{\partial E(y)}{\partial x_j} = \Phi(z)\beta_j \tag{2.20c}$$

$$\frac{\partial E(y \mid y > 0)}{\partial x_j} = \beta_j\left[1 - z\frac{\phi(z)}{\Phi(z)} - \left(\frac{\phi(z)}{\Phi(z)}\right)^2\right] \tag{2.20d}$$

Here, z is a particular value of $x_i\beta/\sigma$, and we are taking the derivatives with respect to the jth x variable (we drop the i subscripts for convenience).[4] In all four cases, the sign of the partial derivative is the same as the sign of β_j.

The partial derivative of $E(y^*)$ with respect to (wrt, for short) x_j is, as noted earlier, simply the corresponding β_j. This is constant, a fact that derives from the linear relationship between y^* and the x variables (as shown in Equation 2.1). So, to refer back to the example with which we began this chapter, the β coefficient for, say, monthly income tells us the degree to which the propensity of individual households to spend on luxury goods changes for a small change in household monthly income, all other things being equal. By contrast, the partial derivatives of $\text{pr}(y > c)$, $E(y)$, and $E(y|y > c)$ wrt x_j all depend on the value of z; thus, they are not linear.

In the case of (b), the β coefficients can be interpreted in the same way as those obtained from a probit analysis, except that we must divide the βs by σ. This follows because, whereas σ is not estimable separately from the βs in a probit, it is separately estimable in a Tobit model. Thus, in our example, this tells us how a small change in one of the explanatory variables (say, income) affects the probability of a household spending anything at all on luxury goods. As with the probit, however, the effect of a change in x_j on the probability is greatest when the probability is around one half, and least when the probability approaches either zero or one (see Aldrich & Nelson, 1984, p. 43). This result follows because the partial derivative is given by the relevant β coefficient weighted by the standard normal density function, ϕ_i, which approaches zero when the corresponding probability approaches zero or one and takes its maximum value when the probability equals one half.

In the case of the partial derivative of $E(y)$, this is equal to the relevant coefficient, β_j, weighted by $\Phi_i(z)$, which is the probability that an observation, with a given set of x values, is uncensored. The greater is this probability, the bigger is the change in $E(y_i)$ for a change in x_j. This would seem intuitively sensible, because if the probability of y_i exceeding c is very small (that is, if y_i^* is very much less than c), a small change in x_{ij} will have little or no effect on $E(y_i)$ because y_i^* will remain below c and so y_i will remain at zero. So, this derivative tells us how observed expenditure on luxury goods changes given a small change in one of the x variables when all the other x variables remain unchanged.

Finally, the partial derivative of the expected value of y, conditional on y exceeding the threshold, tells us, in the example we have been using, the effect of a small change in one of the x variables on the amount spent on luxury goods among those households who spend at least something in this way. As the formula shows, this derivative is equal to the relevant β coefficient, weighted by the expression in square brackets. This latter expression is always positive, and it increases as z increases. Thus, those who spend more on luxury goods will respond more to a change in one of the x variables than will those who spend less.

One interesting and useful decomposition of the Tobit partial derivative was suggested by McDonald and Moffit (1980). They begin from Equation

2.8 for the expected value of y, and they note that the partial derivative of this with respect to one of the x variables can be written[5]

$$\frac{\partial E(y)}{\partial x_j} = \Phi(z)\left(\frac{\partial E(y \mid y > 0)}{\partial x_j}\right) + E(y \mid y > 0)\left(\frac{\partial \Phi(z)}{\partial x_j}\right), \qquad (2.21)$$

which is equal to

$$= \Phi(z) \times \beta_j\left[1 - z\frac{\phi(z)}{\Phi(z)} - \left(\frac{\phi(z)}{\Phi(z)}\right)^2\right] + \left[x_i'\beta + \sigma\frac{\phi}{\Phi}\right] \times \phi(z)\frac{\beta_j}{\sigma} \qquad (2.22)$$

The important point that McDonald and Moffit make, however, is that this expression for the total change in y can be split into two parts: The first is the change in y among those observations above the censoring threshold, weighted by the probability of being above the threshold (this is the first part of Equation 2.22); and the second is the change in the probability of being above the threshold, weighted by the expected value of y for those observations above the threshold. This allows us to decompose Tobit effects. So, in the case of expenditure on luxury goods, we could decompose the effect of each explanatory variable into two "subeffects": first, the effect of this variable on expenditure, given that some amount is spent on luxury goods; and second, its effect on the probability of spending any amount at all on luxury goods. In our example using simulated data, if we calculate the McDonald and Moffit decomposition using the mean value of x in our sample, we get the following result. First, the derivative of $E(y)$ wrt x is equal to Φ_i (evaluated at $x_i = .45513$), multiplied by β (= 2.125), which equals 1.278. This can be decomposed into .532, because of the change in $E(y \mid y > 0)$ evaluated at Φ_i; and .746, because of the change in the probability of being above the zero threshold, evaluated at the mean value of $E(y \mid y > 0)$. In this case, then, the change in the probability is the slightly more significant effect on $E(y)$, accounting for about 58% of the total change in the value of y. The interested reader is referred to the McDonald and Moffit (1980) paper for several empirical applications of this decomposition.

2.6 An Empirical Example

Honohan and Nolan (1993) used the Tobit model to investigate the percentage share of financial assets in the total wealth of households in the

TABLE 2.3
Factors Influencing the Percentage of Household Wealth Held
in Financial Assets (*t* values in parentheses)

Explanatory Variables	OLS	Tobit
	Method	
Constant	6.26 (3.3)	−7.47 (2.8)
Wealth[a]	−0.69 (6.0)	−0.18 (1.1)
Wealth-squared	−0.003 (2.5)	−0.003 (1.6)
Income[b]	0.006 (2.5)	0.016 (5.3)
Urban	6.14 (5.9)	7.35 (5.1)
Male-headed household	4.09 (3.0)	3.71 (2.0)
Professional socioeconomic group	2.92 (2.1)	6.20 (3.3)
Self-employed	−4.56 (2.3)	−4.87 (1.9)

a. Measured in units of 10,000 Irish pounds.
b. Gross total annual household income, measured in units of 100 Irish pounds.
Source. Honohan and Nolan (1993), p. 83.

Republic of Ireland. Their sample comprised 3,089 households, of which 2,121 had some of their wealth in the form of financial assets (i.e., stocks, bonds, and savings). They sought to explain the share of wealth held as financial assets in terms of the household's total wealth (measured in Irish pounds), its total gross annual income, its location (urban or rural, entered into the model as a dummy variable), the sex of the household head (a dummy variable taking the value 1 for a male-headed household), whether the head of the household was a professional employee, and whether the head of the household was self-employed. Total wealth was modeled as a quadratic term, so a variable equal to the square of total wealth was also entered into the model. Table 2.3 gives the results of fitting this model to all 3,089 households, using OLS and Tobit.

Perhaps the most surprising result is the negative coefficients for both wealth and wealth-squared in the OLS regression, suggesting that the share of total wealth in financial assets declines with increasing wealth. However, in the Tobit this effect disappears, with neither variable reaching statistical significance—a result that seems somewhat more plausible. Conversely, in the Tobit, the effects of income and being in the professional socioeconomic group are much stronger. The overall low level of financial assets held by households (constituting only 8% of total wealth) (Honohan & Nolan, 1993, p. 17) contrasts sharply with the widespread ownership of housing (55% of total wealth) and even farmland (25%). It seems that financial assets are invested in only by those with relatively high levels of disposable income.

The Tobit coefficients reported in Table 2.3 should be interpreted in relation to an underlying, unobserved latent variable that might be considered as the household's propensity or capacity to invest in financial assets. Thus, the income coefficient of .016, for example, tells us how a change of one unit in household income affects the propensity to invest in financial assets. On the other hand, the effect of a one-unit change in income on the observed share of wealth in financial assets is given by Equation 2.20c; it thus depends on the value of the other coefficients and the household's value on the corresponding variables. However, if we set $\Phi(z)$ equal to the observed probability of having some financial assets in total wealth (2,121/ 3,089 = .687), then the income effect on the observed share of wealth is rather weaker—equal to .011. This is the expected change in holding of financial assets, given a one-unit change in income, for a household with an average probability of having invested in any financial assets. Even so, this is still greater than the biased and inconsistent OLS estimate of .006. Use of OLS in this case would have led Honohan and Nolan to underestimate the effect of income in influencing households' investment in financial assets.[6]

Notes

1. So, for example, in the case of expectation, the expected value of a discrete random variable, z, is given by

$$\sum_i z_i \, pr(z = z_i) \,,$$

whereas for a continuous variable, y, it is given by

$$\int_{-\infty}^{\infty} y \, f(y) \, dy \,,$$

where f denotes the density function.

2. For a formal statement of the difference between consistency and asymptotic unbiasedness, see Dhrymes (1989, pp. 86-89).

3. Another problem concerns the complexity of the log-likelihood function. If the model we specify contains very complex multivariate integrals, for example, it may be practically unfeasible to estimate it using ML.

4. These four partial derivatives are evaluated under the assumption that $c = 0$. If this is not so, then the partial derivatives in fact remain unchanged, except for Equation 2.20c, to which we must add the extra term $-\phi(z)\beta_j/\sigma$ to take account of the partial effect of a change in x_j on the probability of an observation taking the nonzero threshold value, c.

5. Here, use is being made of the product rule of differentiation, which states that, given a relationship $y = f(x)g(x)$, the derivative of y wrt x is equal to $f(x)g'(x) + f'(x)g(x)$, where $'$ denotes the derivative of a function. The decomposition shown here applies only when $c = 0$. If this does not hold, then an extra term must be added to reflect the effect of a change in x_j on the probability of an observation taking the value c.

6. Unfortunately, Honohan and Nolan (1993) do not report their estimate of the variance of the error term in their Tobit model, and so we cannot calculate the partial derivative of income with respect to the probability of allocating any share of wealth in financial assets.

3. SAMPLE-SELECTION MODELS AND THE TRUNCATED REGRESSION MODEL

One striking feature of the Tobit model is that the same set of variables, with the same coefficients, is held to determine both the probability of truncation and the expected value of the realized dependent variable, conditional on its having been observed. In this chapter, we look at some models where this constraint is relaxed, so that the effects of variables on each of the two steps can be different, and so that different variables can influence each of the steps.

The model introduced by Cragg (1971) weakens one of the central characteristics of the Tobit model. Recall that, in the latter, we have the following expression for the probability of the latent variable exceeding the threshold, c:

$$\text{pr}(y_i^* > c) = \Phi\left(\frac{x_i'\beta}{\sigma}\right). \tag{3.1a}$$

And the expected value of y^* conditional on $\mathbf{x}$ is given by

$$E(y_i^* \mid x_i) = x_i'\beta. \tag{3.1b}$$

Cragg's model retains Equation 3.1b but replaces Equation 3.1a with

$$\text{pr}(y_i^* > c) = \Phi(x_i'\gamma). \tag{3.1c}$$

Comparing the two, we see that the variables affecting this probability remain the same, but now the two parts of the expression (for the probability and the conditional expectation) have different coefficients. These two parts are then estimated separately, under the assumption that the two stages are independent of each other. Cragg introduced this model in the context of the demand for automobiles, the decision of whether or not to purchase a car being independent of the decision about how much to spend having decided to buy one. Another example is provided by Fin and Schmidt (1984): The probability of a fire breaking out in a building may well be a positive function of the building's age, but the value of the damage done by a fire may be a negative function of age.

3.1 Sample-Selection Models

Sample-selection models extend Cragg's model by relaxing the assumption that the two stages are independent. The basic idea of such models is that the outcome variable, y, is only observed if some criterion, defined with respect to a *different* variable, say, z, is met. The simplest form of such a model has two stages: In the first stage, a dichotomous variable z ($= 0$ or 1) determines whether or not y is observed, y being observed only if $z = 1$; in the second stage, we model the expected value of y, conditional on its having been observed.

More formally, let

$$z_i^* = w_i'\alpha + e_i \tag{3.2a}$$

$$z_i = 0 \text{ if } z_i^* \leq 0;$$

$$z_i = 1 \text{ if } z_i^* > 0$$

$$y_i^* = x_i'\beta + u_i \tag{3.2b}$$

$$y_i = y_i^* \text{ if } z_i = 1$$

$$y_i \text{ not observed if } z_i = 0 .$$

In words, we observe z, a dummy variable, which is a realization of an unobserved (or latent) continuous variable, z^*, having a normally distributed, independent error, e, with mean zero and constant variance σ_e^2. For values of $z = 1$, we observe y, which is the observed realization of a second latent variable, y^*, which has a normally distributed, independent error, u, with mean zero and constant variance σ_u^2. The two errors are assumed to have correlation ρ. Thus, the joint distribution of u and e is bivariate normal. The two sets of explanatory variables, $\mathbf{w}$ and $\mathbf{x}$, need not be disjoint and, indeed, in some empirical applications, they are identical. If ρ is assumed to be zero, then we have Cragg's model.

In practice, a nonzero correlation between the error terms is often assumed to arise as a result of the omission of an explanatory variable common to Equations 3.2a and 3.2b. For example, suppose that we are interested in the earnings of people who leave unemployment. The selection equation would focus on the probability of leaving unemployment, and the outcome equation, which applied only to those who left unemployment, would have earnings, or some function of earnings, as its dependent variable. One relevant variable affecting both stages of this process might be "motivation." Those who are better motivated might be more likely to escape from unemployment and to earn more. Because motivation may be difficult to measure in sample surveys, it might not be included in the model. This would then cause the two error terms to have a nonzero correlation.

However, such an interpretation is not correct. Instead, the correlation should be thought of as intrinsic to the model. In other words, we assume $\rho \neq 0$ in the theoretical model that we posit for the population and not simply for the sample in which we may have omitted the measurement of a variable common to $\mathbf{x}$ and $\mathbf{z}$. Thus, whatever is the cause of the correlation between u and e should be inherently unmeasurable. As Berk and Ray (1982) note, "The errors covary *despite* proper model specification. In essence then, both equations are affected (in part) by the same random perturbations (or random perturbations that tend to covary)" (p. 383).

The sample-selection model has been used in many empirical social science studies.[1] If we think hard enough, we can probably find some sort of selection process underlying any piece of social science data. A random sample of the adult population is actually only a random sample of those members of the population who are listed in the sampling frame; so, if the sampling frame is, say, an electoral register, those adults who are not registered cannot be sampled. Does this mean, then, that we should try to correct for any bias that this might induce in our estimation results? In general, the answer is probably no, except in cases where we strongly suspect that failure to register may be nonrandom. This may have been the case in Britain in the late 1980s and early 1990s, when the introduction of a flat-rate poll tax levied on all those on the electoral register may have led to deliberate nonregistration by, for example, relatively poor people. Whether a particular process of sample selection is likely to have substantive effects often will be a matter of judgment, and sometimes we may be able to ignore it.

The problem, in cases depicted by the set-up shown in Equation 3.2, is that estimates of β derived from simply regressing y on x using those observations for which $z = 1$ will be inconsistent and biased (we demonstrate why later). Once again, one way of addressing this problem involves breaking it into two steps. First, we model the probability of an observation being selected; in other words, we model z as a dummy variable, dependent upon the variables w. Then, we examine the expectation of the y variable, conditional on the observations in question having been selected. This entails modeling y as dependent upon variables x but correcting, or allowing, for the fact that y is only observed when $z = 1$.

To carry out the two-step estimation, we use the Heckman procedure. We begin with a probit model for the probability of $z = 1$, estimated using all our observations and yielding coefficient vector α:

$$\text{pr}(z_i = 1) = \Phi(w_i'\alpha).$$

Once again, because α and σ_e are not separately identifiable in the probit, we assume that $\sigma_e = 1$.

The second step is to estimate the expected value of y, conditional on $z = 1$ and on the vector x_i. The steps in deriving this value parallel those for the Tobit case (in Equations 2.5a, 2.5b, and 2.6).

$$E(y_i \mid z = 1, x_i) = x_i'\beta + E(u_i \mid z_i = 1)$$

$$x_i'\beta + E(u_i \mid e_i > w_i'\alpha) \tag{3.3a}$$

To evaluate the conditional expectation of u in Equation 3.3a, we have recourse to another result from statistical theory. This result says that the expected value of one of the variables in a bivariate distribution (in this case, u) censored with respect to the value of the other variable (in this case, e) is given by

$$E(u_i \mid e_i > w_i'\alpha) = \rho\sigma_e\sigma_u \frac{\phi(w_i'\alpha)}{\Phi(w_i'\alpha)}. \tag{3.3b}$$

This expression is more complex than for the Tobit because we are now examining the expected value of u conditional not on u itself exceeding a given value but on the value of a different variable, e. Inserting Equation 3.3b into Equation 3.3a gives us

$$E(y_i \mid z = 1, x_i) = x_i'\beta + \rho\sigma_e\sigma_u\frac{\phi(w_i'\alpha)}{\Phi(w_i'\alpha)}. \tag{3.3c}$$

To estimate this model, we first take the probit results and, for the subsample for whom $z = 1$, we compute the estimate of ϕ_i/Φ_i (the inverse Mill's ratio, once again symbolized by λ_i). Then, for this same subsample, we use OLS to regress y on x_i and on our estimate of λ_i:

$$E(y_i \mid z = 1, x_i) = x_i'\beta + \theta\hat{\lambda}_i. \tag{3.4}$$

This will yield estimates of β and θ. θ is an estimate of ρ times σ_u, which, because $\sigma_e = 1$ is equal to the covariance between u and e (σ_{ue}),

$$\theta = \rho\sigma_u = \frac{\sigma_{ue}}{\sigma_u\sigma_e}\sigma_u = \sigma_{ue}.$$

Recall that our motivation for discussing these models is that we want to acquire good estimates of the effect of the x variables on the dependent variable. So, if we simply take those cases for which we have observations on y and regress y_i on x_i, Equation 3.4 shows that the resulting estimates of the vector β in general will be biased because the variable λ has been omitted. The problem of sample-selection bias thus becomes equivalent to a misspecification problem arising through the omission of a regressor variable. However, there are two situations in which the OLS estimates of β will be unbiased. These are as follows:

1. If $\rho = 0$, this means that θ in Equation 3.4 must also be zero, and thus Equation 3.4 reduces to the usual OLS equation. This corresponds to the situation in which selection and outcome are independent.

2. If the correlation between the estimate of λ and any x variable (say, x_k) is zero, then the OLS estimate of this variable's coefficient, β_k, will be unbiased. This follows from the well-known result concerning the effects of omitted variable misspecification in OLS. Given the missing variable,

λ, the extent of the bias in the estimate of β_k will be equal to the correlation between x_k and λ multiplied by the estimate of θ. If the correlation is zero, so will be the bias (see Johnston, 1972, pp. 168-169; Kmenta, 1971, pp. 393-394).

When we discussed the two-step modeling of the censored regression model in Chapter 2, we noted that the standard errors of the coefficients and the estimate of σ from the outcome equation were incorrect. The same is true in this case. To adjust the estimate of σ_u is relatively easy. Define $\delta_i = -\lambda_i(z_i + \lambda_i)$, where $z_i = \mathbf{w}_i'\alpha$ from the probit step. Then, let s_u be the uncorrected estimate of σ_u from the regression (second) step of the Heckman procedure, and let S be the sum of squared deviations from this regression:

$$S = \sum_1 (y_i - \hat{y}_i)^2,$$

where the sum is taken over all observations for which $z = 1$. The correct asymptotic estimate of σ_u is given by

$$\hat{\sigma}_u = \frac{1}{N}\left[S - \hat{\theta}^2 \sum_{i=1}^{N} \hat{\delta}_i\right]^{1/2} \tag{3.5}$$

where N is the number of observations for which $z = 1$ and θ is the estimated regression coefficient for λ (Greene, 1990, pp. 744-745; Heckman, 1979, p. 157).

The standard errors are incorrect for two reasons: Model 3.4 is heteroscedastic, and the use of an estimate of λ, rather than λ itself, means that the standard errors for the β coefficients will need to take account of the error in the estimate of λ. Unfortunately, the uncorrected (OLS) standard errors can be either larger or smaller than the corrected ones; hence, they cannot be used as lower bounds on the true standard errors. The formula for the correct covariance matrix of the estimates of β and σ_u, V, is given by the matrix equation

$$V = \sigma_u^2 (X^{*'}X^*)^{-1}[X^{*'}(I - \rho^2\Delta)X^* \\ + \rho^2(X^*\Delta W)\Sigma(W'\Delta X^*)](X^{*'}X^*)^{-1} \tag{3.6}$$

The standard errors of the parameter estimates are given by the square root of the diagonal elements of V. Here, X^* is the matrix $[\mathbf{x}:\lambda]$; W is the matrix of explanatory variables from the probit equation; Δ is a matrix with the elements δ_i on its diagonal, zeros elsewhere; I is the identity matrix; and Σ is the asymptotic covariance matrix for the parameters of the probit equation. We estimate ρ by

$$\hat{\rho} = \frac{\hat{\theta}}{\hat{\sigma}_u}. \tag{3.7}$$

Therefore, to correct the standard errors requires some matrix manipulations (Greene, 1981); however, a software package such as LIMDEP (Greene, 1991) makes these corrections automatically.

Alternatively, the model can be estimated using maximum likelihood. To do this, we need to be able to specify the likelihood function. Let $\Phi_i = \Phi(\mathbf{w}_i'\alpha)$; then, all those cases where $z = 0$ contribute $1 - \Phi_i$ to the likelihood. Those cases where $z = 1$ contribute

$$\Phi_i \times \frac{1}{\sigma}\phi(y_i|z_i = 1), \tag{3.8}$$

where σ is the standard deviation of y^* conditional on $z = 1$ and $\phi(y_i \mid z_i = 1)$ is the conditional density function of y^* given $z = 1$. Equation 3.8 is the expression for the probability of being selected multiplied by the density of y conditional on having been selected. To put this into a tractable form for estimation, some further manipulations are needed. These are beyond the scope of this monograph, but they are shown by Amemiya (1984, pp. 31-32). He demonstrates that Equation 3.8 can be written

$$\Phi\left[\frac{\mathbf{w}_i'\alpha + \rho\left(\dfrac{y_i - x_i'\beta}{\sigma_u}\right)}{(1 - \rho^2)^{1/2}}\right] \times \frac{1}{\sigma_u}\Phi\left(\frac{y_i - x_i'\beta}{\sigma_u}\right). \tag{3.9}$$

Inserting the expression for those observations where $z = 0$ and taking logarithms, we arrive at the log-likelihood:

$$L = \sum_0 \log(1 - \Phi_i) + \sum_1 \log \frac{1}{\sqrt{2\pi\sigma_u^2}} - \sum_1 \frac{1}{2\sigma_u^2}(y_i - x_i'\beta)^2 \qquad (3.10)$$

$$+ \sum_1 \log\Phi\left[\frac{w_i'\alpha + \rho\left(\dfrac{y_i - x_i'\beta}{\sigma_u}\right)}{(1 - \rho^2)^{1/2}}\right]$$

One use of the likelihood equation is in showing us the circumstances under which this model reduces to something simpler. Note that if $\rho = 0$, then Equation 3.10 can be split into two parts: a probit for the probability of being selected and an OLS regression for the expected value of y in the selected subsample. Furthermore, because these two parts share no common parameters, they can be estimated separately. This shows that if there is no residual correlation between e and u, the simple OLS approach is adequate. Therefore, it is not the fact that observations on y are only available for a selected sample that causes the difficulty; rather, it is that this selection is not random with respect to y.

We now have three possible approaches to analyzing sample-selected data: a naive OLS, the Heckman two-step estimator, and maximum likelihood (ML). Estimates obtained by OLS will be both biased and inconsistent (these terms were defined in Chapter 2). By contrast, the Heckman two-stage estimators will be consistent. The ML estimators, provided that the appropriate assumptions (as outlined above in our discussion of Equations 3.2a and 3.2b) are met, will be asymptotically unbiased and asymptotically normal, and they will be more efficient than the two-stage estimator. On these grounds, and given the availability of ML routines for this model, ML estimates are generally to be preferred.

As an example, we begin with a setup like that described in Equations 3.2a and 3.2b: Specifically, we have a population in which

$$y_i^* = 1 + 2x_i + u_i \qquad (3.11a)$$

$$z_i^* = 1 + 2w_i + e_i \qquad (3.11b)$$

and

$$z_i = 0 \text{ if } z_i^* \le 0;$$

TABLE 3.1
Estimation Results for Sample Selection Models
Applied to Simulated Data (standard errors in parentheses)

Method	Estimates of			
	α	β	σ_u	ρ_{ue}
1. OLS (for observations where $z = 1$)	1.2316 (0.0527)	1.9077 (0.0537)	1.7738	—
2. Heckman two-step method (uncorrected)	1.0262 (0.0570)	1.9620 (0.0527)	1.7252	0.7266
3. Heckman two-step method (corrected)	1.0262 (0.0585)	1.9620 (0.0529)	1.7870	0.7014
4. Maximum likelihood	1.0035 (0.0552)	1.9801 (0.0522)	1.7889 (0.0384)	0.7626 (0.0435)

$$z_i = 1 \text{ if } z_i^* > 0;$$

$$y_i = y_i^* \text{ if } z_i = 1;$$

$$y_i \text{ not observed if } z_i = 0,$$

where

$$\sigma_e \sim N(0,1); \sigma_u \sim N(0,1.8028); \rho_{e,u} = .8321.$$

We also set the correlation between x and w at .2425. We then draw a random sample of 2,000 observations from this population, with the purpose of using the sample data to estimate the parameters α (the intercept in Equation 3.11a), β, σ_u, and ρ. Table 3.1 shows the results of a number of ways of doing this.

The first row presents estimates based on OLS using the 1,173 selected cases for which we have a valid value of y. We have no estimate of ρ in this case because it is assumed to be zero. Row 2 shows the Heckman two-stage method estimates, as does Row 3, the difference between them being that the latter presents corrected standard errors and estimate of σ. In both of these cases, ρ is calculated as shown in Equation 3.7. The final row presents the ML estimates. It is immediately evident that, in this case, both the two-step method and ML bring the estimates of both α and β closer to their known population values, and the corrected two-step and ML methods also improve the estimates of σ_u and ρ. However, the ML estimates have smaller standard errors than do the two-step estimates. For all four parameters, the best results are obtained using maximum likelihood. Whether this will always be so, however, is an issue we will deal with in some detail in Chapter 5.

3.2 Parameter Interpretation

As in the Tobit case, there are several ways in which the parameter estimates of this model can be interpreted.

1. The probability that an observation is selected into the sample is given by the coefficients from the probit part of the model. In the ML approach, these are estimated simultaneously with all the other coefficients in the model.

$$\text{pr}(z_i^* > 0) = \text{pr}(z_i = 1) = \Phi(w_i'\alpha). \qquad (3.12a)$$

The derivative of this probability with respect to a given **w** variable, w_k, is simply (dropping the i subscripts for convenience)

$$\frac{\partial pr(z = 1)}{\partial w_k} = \phi(g)\alpha_k. \qquad (3.12b)$$

Here, g denotes a particular value of $w_i'\alpha$.

2. The expected value of the latent variable, y^*, is given by

$$E(y_i^*|x_i) = x_i'\beta, \qquad (3.13a)$$

and the derivative of this with respect to a given **x** variable—x_k—is simply β_k. Note that this is not an estimate of the marginal effect on the observed y values, but rather of the marginal effect on the expected value in the population as a whole.

3. The expected value of y among the selected sample is given by

$$E(y_i|z = 1, x_i) = x_i'\beta + \rho\sigma_u\hat{\lambda}. \qquad (3.14a)$$

The derivative of y with respect to x_k is then given as follows:

$$\frac{\partial E(y \mid z = 1)}{\partial x_k} = \beta_k - \alpha_k \rho \sigma_u \left[g \frac{\phi(g)}{\Phi(g)} - \left(\frac{\phi(g)}{\Phi(g)} \right)^2 \right]. \tag{3.14b}$$

This expression is very similar to Equation 2.20d for the Tobit model, except that it includes the coefficient α_k, which, in this instance, measures the effect of x_k in determining the probability of selection. This term is obviously relevant only if x_k appears as one of the w as well as one of the x variables. If, as in our simulated example, it does not, then its effect on y is simply captured by β_k. But if it does, then it will have two kinds of effect: a direct effect, through β_k, and an indirect effect, because a change in x_k also changes the estimated value of λ. But in Equation 3.14b, the quantity $\rho \sigma_u \{ g[\phi(g)/\Phi(g)] - [\phi(g)/\Phi(g)]^2 \}$ is always positive, and therefore the sign of these two effects is different. Hence, if the variable in question does have a positive influence on both the probability of selection and the expected value of the outcome, neglecting the second part of the derivative will overstate its impact on y.

One interpretation that can be given to the Tobit coefficients, but that would not be sensible in the sample-selection case, relates to the unconditional expected value of the realized variable, y. Recall that, in the Tobit case, this included all the values of y fixed at the censoring value; but in the sample selection case we know nothing at all about the values of y among the unselected observations.

3.3 Some Practical Issues

Methods for censored and sample-selected data are not without their problems, and Chapter 5 deals with these in some detail. There are, however, a number of practical issues that we might mention here. The first of these concerns identification. As we noted above, some empirical studies using the Heckman estimator have employed the same explanatory variables in modeling both the selection and outcome mechanisms. Other studies have used a set of variables in the outcome equation that includes all the variables used in the selection equation. In such cases, the parameters of the outcome equation are then identified only because of the nonlinearity of the probit equation. Were both equations linear, then, given the nonzero correlation between the error terms, the model would not be identified. This is easily seen in the two-step version: If all the w variables also appear in **x,** then given a linear selection equation, the estimate of λ would be a linear function of a subset of the **x** variables. As a general rule, it is not a good idea to rely on the probit's nonlinearity for identification. It is much better to place restrictions on the coefficients, such that a variable that affects the selection stage has no effect on the outcome. This will ensure identifiability, although which restrictions are appropriate will depend upon the conceptual model that underlies the analysis. There can be little justification for introducing constraints purely for the purpose of identifying the model. In practice, reliance on the nonlinearity of the probit can result in barely identified, and thus unstable, parameter estimates. For example, if, in the simulation reported above, we replace w in Equation 3.11b with x, then, in the corrected two-step approach, the sample correlations between the parameter estimates of α, β, and θ are all around .8. It is a wise policy always to examine the correlations between the estimated parameters of a model. This is essential if reliance on the nonlinearity of the probit is being used for identification.

Another problem that can arise in the two-step model concerns the estimate of ρ. Because it is calculated as the ratio of two quantities—as shown in Equation 3.7—there is no guarantee that it will fall in the interval −1 to 1. If this happens, there is little that can be done beyond a careful examination of the model for possible sources of misspecification.

3.4 Empirical Examples

Examples of ML methods used to model sample-selection bias are much less common than uses of the Heckman two-step method. A good example of this is provided by Hagan and Parker (1985). They investigated the factors associated with the severity of sentence (measured by an 11-point scale) handed down to white-collar criminals. The selection problem occurred because their sample comprised all those charged with such a crime: Of these, 63% were convicted and thus sentenced. In modeling the probability of conviction, Hagan and Parker's probit included 10 explanatory variables. Of these, only three were significant (at the conventional .05 level) (Hagan & Parker, 1985, p. 309). Exactly the same set of variables was then used in the outcome equation. Without correcting for selection bias, only one variable was significant: This was a dummy for "Type of Charge," which was found to have a strong positive effect on sentence severity (estimate of $\beta = 3.307$ with standard error $= 0.402$). When the inverse Mill's ratio estimate was added to the outcome equation, a number of coefficients changed sign, but none became significant. The coefficient for "Type of Charge" barely changed (3.542 with standard error = 0.443), and the inverse Mill's ratio estimate itself was not significant, having a standard error almost as large as its coefficient (–2.905 with standard error = 2.306). The biggest effect of its inclusion was to change the constant term from 8.63 to 5.14. Hagan and Parker (1985) conclude that "there is little evidence that looking only at convicted offenders will bias our analysis" (p. 309).

It is not unusual to find studies in which inclusion of the inverse Mill's ratio estimate in the outcome equation is found to have little impact on the coefficients of the other variables in the model and/or the inverse Mill's ratio instrument's coefficient (that is, the estimate of the covariance between u and e) is itself found to be nonsignificant (e.g., Allison & Long, 1987; England, Farkas, Kilbourne, & Dou, 1988; Sanders & Nee, 1987). By contrast, Tienda, Smith, and Ortiz (1988), in a study of the determinants of earnings of men and women, found highly significant coefficients for the estimated inverse Mill's ratio in their analyses. Here, selection bias occurred because the analysis was undertaken on a subsample (those employees with nonzero wages or salary income) of the USA Public Use Census samples for 1970 and 1980. In this case, the probit equation included 15 explanatory variables, of which the majority were significant (Tienda et al., 1988, p. 208). The outcome earnings equation contained 12 explanatory variables, and only 5 variables were common to both equations. For both men and women, the estimated inverse Mill's ratio variable had a significant coefficient and, although Tienda et al. do not present their uncorrected earnings equations, this suggests that failure to correct for sample selection might well have biased their parameter estimates.

In comparing these studies, it may indeed be the case that selection bias is not a problem in modeling sentence severity, whereas it is in modeling earnings. However, the different results of these studies may also owe something to what seems to be the greater explanatory power of the probit equation in the latter case and the fact that, unlike Hagan and Parker, Tienda et al. did not rely on the nonlinearity of the probit for identification in the outcome equation. These are issues that we will return to in more detail in Chapter 5.

3.5 Truncated Regression Models

In censored and sample-selected samples, we lack information on the values of y for observations that fail to meet some criterion; nevertheless, we have the full set of information on the explanatory variables for all observations. Thus, we can say that although y itself is truncated, the samples are, respectively, censored or sample selected. By contrast, a sample is said to be truncated if we lack information not only on the values of y for observations that do not meet some criterion but also on the values of the explanatory variables for these observations. In this case, our two-step approach is no longer applicable because we do not have the data to model the first, or selection, step. Nevertheless, we can attempt to model the outcome equation, as follows.

We begin by assuming that

$$y_i^* = x_i'\beta + u_i \tag{3.15}$$

and $u \sim N(0,\sigma^2)$. In our sample, we observe y ($= y^*$) only when $y_i^* < c$. If y is income, then c might be the defined poverty line income. So we need to estimate

$$E(y_i|y_i < c, x_i) = E(y_i \mid u_i \leq c - x_i'\beta) . \tag{3.16}$$

Using the results in Appendix A, we can write

$$E(y_i|y_i < c, x_i) = x_i'\beta - \sigma\frac{\phi_i(m)}{\Phi_i(m)}$$

$$= x_i'\beta - \sigma\hat{\lambda}_i(m) \tag{3.17}$$

$$\text{where } m = \frac{c - x_i'\beta}{\sigma} .$$

We can see at once in Equation 3.17 that ignoring truncation and simply regressing the observed y values on x will lead to biased estimates of β because of the omission of the estimated λ. However, in the earlier two-step approach to the Tobit, we could first estimate the inverse Mill's ratio using a probit and then enter it into the outcome equation as a new variable; we lack the information to do this here. Therefore, the two-step method is not feasible, but ML is. Indeed, the log-likelihood for this model simply consists of those parts of the Tobit log-likelihood that relate to the uncensored observations and for which we have information that allows us to include them. Recall that the uncensored observations contributed two parts to the Tobit log-likelihood: the probability of being uncensored (which we cannot now estimate) and a part corresponding to the density function for the truncated normal and shown in Equation 2.14c. It is this that we use. We replace Φ_i in that equation with $\Phi_i(m)$ to give the following expression for the likelihood:

$$\prod \frac{1}{\sigma} \frac{\phi[(y_i - x_i'\beta)/\sigma]}{\Phi_i(m)}. \tag{3.18}$$

This yields, for the log-likelihood,

$$L = \sum \log\frac{1}{\sqrt{2\pi\sigma^2}} - \sum \frac{1}{2\sigma^2}(y_i - x_i'\beta)^2 - \sum \log\Phi\left(\frac{c - x_i'\beta}{\sigma}\right). \tag{3.19}$$

There is no reason why c should be constant; it could be subscripted equally well with an i to indicate that it varies over observations.

The truncated regression model is encountered less frequently than either the censored or sample-selection model. Common examples of its use arise from particular kinds of sampling schemes. If we sample only low-income households or households falling below a defined poverty line, we will have a truncated sample of household incomes. A well-known example of this is found in the work of Hausman and Wise (1977).

To illustrate the model, we turn once again to some simulated data. Suppose that the gross relationship between parental socioeconomic status and pupils' performance in a college entrance exam, y, is given by

$$y_i = 75 + 1.5x_i + u_i, \tag{3.20}$$

where x is parental socioeconomic status and u is normally distributed with a zero mean and standard deviation of 25. We have data from a sample of 350 students who are currently enrolled in the college. Because only those who score at least 125 on the entrance test are admitted to the college, our sample is left truncated. If we ignore the truncation of the data and simply perform an OLS regression on our sample, we get estimates of α, β, and σ of 102.60 (3.36), 1.157 (0.05), and 22.535, respectively (standard errors in parentheses). These estimates are both biased and inconsistent, and their values are all some considerable distance from the (in this case) known population values. However, using the log-likelihood given in Equation 3.19 to estimate the truncated regression model gives estimates of 72.43 (6.36), 1.514 (0.08), and 25.721 (1.294) for α, β, and σ, respectively, all of which are very close to their true values.

The estimate of β derived from the truncated regression model has the usual partial derivative interpretation. That is, it tells us the expected change in the value of y for a small change in the value of x. Because Equation 3.20 characterizes the whole population, this interpretation of β holds for the entire population and not simply for those cases in which y exceeds the truncation threshold.

Note

1. We referred to some of these in Chapter 1. Stolzenberg and Relles (1990, Table 1) provide a list of recent papers in the *American Sociological Review* that use the Heckman technique to correct for sample-selection bias.

4. EXTENSIONS OF THE BASIC MODELS

It is relatively easy to develop more elaborate models of censoring and sample selection. For example, we might specify the outcome equation to take account of situations in which the dependent variable is measured as a dichotomy rather than as a continuous variable. An illustration of this would be a model in which we were interested in whether or not married people divorced but a potential selection bias problem existed because not all the people in our sample were married and could not, therefore, have been at risk of divorce. Our selection step would thus deal with the married/not married dichotomy, whereas the outcome would seek to model the probability of divorce, conditional on having been married. Another possible elaboration concerns the very common situation in which we have outcome measures relating both to the selected and the nonselected sample, as in the case of evaluations of labor market programs where we may have information on the earnings not only of a group who participated in such a program but also on the earnings of those who did not.

Similarly, the selection stage might also be made more elaborate. When we study social processes, we frequently find that they involve a succession of selections such that a cohort that starts out on the process gradually diminishes in size. Education is a case in point: Students drop out of the educational system at various points, so that those who remain to the highest level—to earn a PhD, say—are only a very small percentage of the cohort who entered the system at age 4 or 5. The same is true of the criminal justice system: Of all those arrested, only a proportion are charged, and of these only some will be found guilty, of whom only a fraction will receive a custodial sentence. If such processes culminate in the realization of some outcome measure (such as length of custodial sentence), one way of conceptualizing them might be as a succession of sample-selection stages, with the final stage leading either to a censored or sample-selected outcome.

The range of possible models that involves censoring and/or sample selection of the outcome is very great indeed. In some cases, these more elaborate models can be estimated using two-step techniques (Amemiya, 1979; Maddala, 1983, chaps. 6 and 8), but these are correspondingly more complex. Maximum likelihood (ML) estimators are usually preferable not least because they have a range of desirable properties not always shared by two-step estimators. However, although we could probably specify the log-likelihood for any such complex sample selection or censoring model, our capacity to estimate its parameters would be restricted by practical considerations. We could certainly write a log-likelihood that involved the evaluation of a trivariate or even higher-order integral, but we might experience considerable difficulty finding a program that would carry this out. In addition, although it is known that the Tobit log-likelihood, for example, is strictly concave and thus has a single, global maximum, this may not be the case for a "nonstandard" likelihood. It may have local maxima, with the attendant danger that the estimation routine will converge to a nonmaximum-likelihood solution. Furthermore, in a particular instance, the log-likelihood function may be quite flat, making convergence slow and the parameter estimates very unstable. Therefore, one should approach such models with caution. Be prepared to estimate the model several times with different starting values of the parameters to guard against local maxima, and be wary of models in which the parameter estimates change erratically from iteration to iteration or in which convergence of the log-likelihood function is highly nonmonotonic (see Eliason, 1994, p. 45).

In this chapter, we restrict attention to two sorts of more elaborate models. In the first part of the chapter we examine some censored regression models in which the selection process gives rise to multiple truncation thresholds of the dependent variable. As we will see, such models demonstrate the close relationship that exists between censored regression and some other important econometric models, such as the ordered probit used to estimate regressions when the dependent variable is ordinal. In the second part of the chapter we return to an issue on which we briefly touched in Chapter 1, namely, situations in which the selection and outcome stages can no longer be considered to be sequential. Rather, both may be viewed as endogenous to some particular process, such that the two stages have to be treated as simultaneous.

4.1 Selection Processes With Multiple Thresholds

In the basic censored regression (Tobit) model, there is one censoring threshold, c, that is constant across all observations. However, as we noted in Chapter 3 in our treatment of the truncated regression model, c could equally be a variable, varying in value across observations. This would entail only a minor change to the log-likelihood. Another elaboration of the model involves the use of two or more thresholds. For example, we may observe the exact values of a variable only if its value falls between an upper and a lower limit. This might arise in commodity trading (as noted by Maddala, 1983, pp. 160-161), where the existence of daily limits on the movement of prices means that we observe only the doubly truncated part of the underlying latent price, y^*. The same is true of exchange rates that are allowed to float within a predetermined band (as in the European Exchange Rate Mechanism). We assume that y^* is the underlying latent exchange rate between two currencies, but we observe it only provided that it falls between the upper and lower exchange rate limits.

In general, we have

$$y_i^* = x_i'\beta + u_i \qquad (4.1)$$

$$u_i \sim N(0, \sigma^2)$$

and

$$y_i = y_i^* \text{ if } c_1 \leq y_i^* \leq c_2$$

$$y_i = c_1 \text{ if } c_1 > y_i^*$$

$$y_i = c_2 \text{ if } c_2 < y_i^* \qquad (4.2)$$

In this case, the likelihood function has three parts. First, those observations for which the value of the latent variable falls below the lower threshold, c_1, contribute a term relating to the probability of not exceeding the lower limit. Second, those observations for which the value of the latent variable exceeds the upper threshold, c_2, contribute a term relating to the probability of exceeding the upper limit. Third, those observations for which we have an exact value of the variable y contribute a term equal to the probability of falling between the thresholds multiplied by the conditional density function of y^*. Once again, using the results in Appendix A, we begin by writing the probability that the latent variable, y^*, exceeds a given threshold, c_m:

$$\text{pr}(y_i^* > c_m) = \text{pr}(x_i'\beta + u_i > c_m)$$
$$= \text{pr}(u_i > c_m - x_i'\beta)$$
$$= 1 - \Phi\left(\frac{c_m - x_i'\beta}{\sigma}\right)$$

and we denote

$$\Phi\left(\frac{c_m - x_i'\beta}{\sigma}\right) = \Phi_i(c_m)$$

for short. Note that we use this abbreviation throughout this chapter.

The probability that $y^* > c_1$ is therefore $1 - \Phi(c_1)$, and so the probability that $y^* < c_2$ is thus $\Phi(c_2)$. Both of these expressions are used in the log-likelihood. We observe y^* exactly only where y^* falls between the two thresholds. The probability of this is equal to the probability that $y^* < c_2$ minus the probability that $y^* < c_1$:

$$\text{pr}(c_1 \leq y_i^* \leq c_2) = \Phi_i(c_2) - \Phi_i(c_1).$$

For these cases, we also require the conditional density function for y^*, which has, as its denominator, the same expression. So, after canceling, cases where y^* is observed exactly contribute the same term as in the simple Tobit case. Thus, the complete log-likelihood is

$$L = \sum_{y_i = c_1} \log[\Phi_i(c_1)] + \sum_{y_i = c_2} \log[1 - \Phi_i(c_2)] \qquad (4.3)$$
$$+ \sum_{y_i = y_i^*} \log\frac{1}{\sqrt{2\pi\sigma^2}} - \sum_{y_i = y_i^*} \log\frac{1}{2\sigma^2}(y_i - x_i'\beta)^2.$$

This log-likelihood is very similar to that for the ordinary Tobit. There are four useful expected values that we can use the model to compute. First, the expected value of y, conditional on its falling between the two thresholds, is given by

$$E(y_i|c_1 \le y_1 \le c_2) = x_i'\beta + E(u_i|c_1 - x_i'\beta \le u_i \le c_2 - x_i'\beta) \qquad (4.4a)$$

$$= x_i'\beta + \sigma_u \left[\frac{\phi_i(c_1) - \phi_i(c_2)}{\Phi_i(c_2) - \Phi_i(c_1)} \right].$$

So, in the example of exchange rates, this would tell us the expected value of the exchange rate conditional on its being within the exchange rate band. This expression uses the standard statistical result for the expected value of a doubly truncated, random normal variable. To understand the derivation of the conditional expectation of u, recall from Appendix A that in the singly truncated case, the conditional expectation is given by

$$E(u_i|u_i \le c - x_i'\beta) = \sigma \frac{-\phi_i(c)}{\Phi_i(c)}.$$

Because $c_2 - x_i'\beta > c_1 - x_i'\beta$, we can write

$$\text{pr}(c_1 - x_i'\beta \le u_i \le c_2 - x_i'\beta) = \text{pr}(u_i \le c_2 - x_i'\beta) - \text{pr}(u_i \le c_1 - x_i'\beta) \qquad (4.4b)$$

$$= \Phi_i(c_2) - \Phi_i(c_1).$$

This is then the denominator of the conditional expectation of the doubly truncated u. The numerator then follows immediately as

$$\sigma\{-\phi_i(c_2) - [-\phi_i(c_1)]\}.$$

Putting the numerator and denominator together and rearranging yields the latter part of Equation 4.4a.

The unconditional expected value of the observed y is derived by applying a slight extension of Equation 1.1:

$$E(y_i) = \text{pr}(y_i = c_1)c_1 + \text{pr}(y_i = c_2)c_2 + \text{pr}(c_1 \le y_i \le c_2) \times E(y_i|c_1 \le y_i \le c_2).$$

In words, the expected value of the observed variable, y, is equal to the sum of its expected values in all three cases (when y equals either of the limits or when it falls between them) weighted by the probability that each of these cases occurs. So, in our example, this is simply the expected value of the observed exchange rate.

Note that the final part of this expression is identical to Equation 4.4a; so, after canceling, we have

$$E(y_i) = \Phi_i(c_1) \times c_i + [1 - \Phi_i(c_2)] \times c_2 \tag{4.4c}$$
$$+ [\Phi_i(c_2) - \Phi_i(c_1)] \times x_i'\beta + \sigma_u[\phi_i(c_1) - \phi_i(c_2)].$$

Third, the expected value of the latent or underlying exchange rate, y^*, is simply given by $x_i'\beta$, and the βs have their usual partial derivative interpretation with respect to the latent exchange rate. Finally, we can compute three expected probabilities: exceeding the lower threshold, given by $1 - \Phi(c_1)$; not exceeding the upper threshold, given by $\Phi(c_2)$; and falling between the two thresholds, given by Equation 4.4b. The interpretation of the β parameters with respect to these probabilities is the same as in the Tobit case (Chapter 2).

Although this model is useful in its own right, our main reason for introducing it is to show its close links with some other models of interest to social scientists. The model we have just described might arise when we collect continuous data (such as income) and we group the highest and lowest incomes in bands. Typically, however, surveys ask not for exact annual income but, rather, respondents are given a series of income bands and asked into which they fall. To model an income equation using such data requires only minor modifications to Equation 4.3 (see Stewart, 1983). In such a case, we do not have any observations of y^* itself; rather, we know that a given respondent's income is greater than some value and less than another. That is,

$$y_i = 0 \text{ if } y_i^* < c_1$$

$$y_i = 1 \text{ if } c_1 \le y_i^* \le c_2$$

$$\cdots$$

$$y_i = M \text{ if } y_i^* > c_M.$$

The log-likelihood function is then made up of expressions for the probability of observing each value of y. If we assume that the relationship between unobserved income, y^*, and the vector x is given by Equation 4.1,[1] then the log-likelihood is as follows:

$$L = \sum_{y=1} \log[\Phi_i(c_1)] + \sum_{y=2} \log[\Phi_i(c_2) - \Phi_i(c_1)] \qquad (4.5)$$

$$+ \ldots \sum_{y=M} \log[1 - \Phi_i(c_M)]$$

and the estimates of the vector β tell us how the x variables are related to the unobserved, continuous income measure, y^*.

A final elaboration of this model arises if we assume that we know only the rank order of incomes in our sample. In this case, we can modify Equation 4.5 to yield the "ordered probit" model (McKelvey & Zavoina, 1976; see also Maddala, 1983, pp. 46-49), where the thresholds, or cutoff points, are parameters to be estimated. Because we now no longer have sufficient information to identify σ separately, we define $d_m = c_m/\sigma$, for $m = 1$, ... M, and $\gamma = \beta/\sigma$ and write

$$\Phi(d_m) = \Phi(d_m - x_i'\gamma).$$

If, in Equation 4.5, we replace $\Phi_i(c_m)$ with this expression, it yields the log-likelihood for the ordered probit. Here, the parameters to be estimated are the vector γ and the d_m values. If we include a constant term in x, then one of the d_m values will not be identified. So, for example, if we have five intervals with four cutoff points, the inclusion of the constant term will allow us to estimate only three of them. The first interval will then run from $-\infty$ to 0, the second from 0 to d_1, and so on until the fifth interval, which runs from d_3 to ∞. The model of Equation 4.5 obviously has wide applicability whenever continuous data are collected in bands rather than exactly, whereas the ordered probit has many possible applications in regressions that have an ordinal dependent variable whose values may be assumed to be realizations of an underlying normally distributed variable.

4.2 Sample-Selection Models With
Endogenous Selection and Outcome

Imagine that we have data on a sample of adults, some of whom have a job and some of whom do not. We would like to model the relationship between wages and a vector of x variables. The two are related in the population according to

$$\log(wage) = y_i^* = x_i'\beta + u_i, \tag{4.6}$$

and we make the usual assumptions about u—that is, normally distributed with mean zero and constant variance, σ_u^2. We also assume that our sample observations are independent. We observe y^* only in those cases where the person has a job. Assume that all individuals have a reservation wage, v_i^*, and that they take a job only if they can earn at least as much as v_i^*. We do not observe v^* directly but we know that it can be written as

$$v_i^* = w_i'\alpha + e_i . \tag{4.7}$$

We make the usual assumptions about the error term, e, and $\mathbf{w}$ is a vector of observed variables. We also assume that $\rho(e,u) \neq 0$.

We define $z = 1$ if the individual has a job, $z = 0$ otherwise, and

$$y_i = y_i^* \text{ if } z_i = 1$$

$$y_i \text{ not observed if } z_i = 0.$$

Now, however, if we try to apply our usual two-step approach to the problem, we encounter some difficulties. Specifically,

$$\text{pr}(z_i = 1) = \text{pr}(y_i^* \geq v_i^*) = \text{pr}(y_i^* - w_i'\alpha > e_i) . \tag{4.8}$$

Thus, the decision of whether or not to take a job[2] depends upon the latent wage, y^*, so one cannot view realistically the decision about whether or not to take a job as being prior to the wage offer. Rather, the two steps must be considered to be simultaneous.

The likelihood for this model has two parts. Those who do not work contribute a term that relates to the probability that $v^* > y^*$. This is

$$\mathrm{pr}(v_i{}^* > y_i{}^*) = \mathrm{pr}(w_i'\alpha + e_i > x_i'\beta + u_i) \qquad (4.9)$$

$$= \mathrm{pr}(e_i - u_i > x_i'\beta - w_i'\alpha) \,.$$

But because $e - u$ is normally distributed with variance given by

$$\sigma^2 = \sigma_u^2 + \sigma_e^2 - 2\sigma_{ue},$$

we can write Equation 4.9 as

$$\Phi\!\left(\frac{w_i'\alpha - x_i'\beta}{\sigma}\right). \qquad (4.10)$$

The other part of the likelihood concerns those who have a job; in other words, those for whom the condition shown in Equation 4.8 is met. In our earlier discussion of the sample-selection model likelihood, we noted that cases in which y was observed contributed a term made up of a conditional density function multiplied by the probability of having been selected. Here, things are a little more complicated. This time, these observations' contribution to the likelihood is the *bivariate* density function of u and e, truncated with respect to e at the value $y_i{}^* - w_i'\alpha$. That is,

$$\int_{-\infty}^{y_i - w_i'\alpha} f(u_i, e_i)\,de \,, \qquad (4.11)$$

where $f(a,b)$ denotes the bivariate density function of two normally distributed random variables, a and b. Equation 4.11 tells us that we are here focusing on that part of the joint density function of u and e in which the condition $e < y_i - w_i'\alpha$ holds—which is, of course, exactly the condition specified in Equation 4.8 to distinguish those who have an observed wage from those who do not.

As Maddala (1983, p. 76) shows, this part of the likelihood can be simplified to yield

$$\sum_{z=1}\left[\log\frac{1}{\sqrt{2\pi\sigma_u^2}} - \frac{1}{2\sigma_u^2}(y_i - x_i'\beta)^2\right. \tag{4.12}$$

$$\left. + \log\Phi\left(\frac{\sigma_u^2}{\sigma_e^2\sigma_u^2 - \sigma_{eu}^2}\left(y_i - w_i\alpha - \frac{\sigma_{eu}^2}{\sigma_u^2}(y_i - x_i'\beta)\right)\right)\right]$$

where σ_{eu}^2 is the squared covariance between u and e.

The complete log-likelihood for this model is then the sum of Equation 4.12 (where the summation is, as noted, taken over all those who have a job) and Equation 4.8 (taken over all those who do not have a job). It is well known that for this model to be identified, the correlation between e and u must be zero and/or there must exist a variable that is included in x but not in w.

Although the sequential two-step approach is no longer applicable, the likelihood function for this model still contains a contribution from the unselected cases and a contribution from the selected cases. The log-likelihood is similar to that for the basic sample selection model, given in Equation 3.10. The added complication arises because, in this case, we are dealing with two endogenous variables, one of which is truncated. Models giving rise to this log-likelihood function have been extensively used in studying labor supply issues since the early work of Gronau (1974), Lewis (1974), and Heckman (1974). It can be extended quite readily to include various additional sources of truncation and sample selection, as Maddala (1983, pp. 200-202) shows.

Notes

1. Given that the dependent variable is income, in practice, we would usually take y^* to be some transformation of income, such as its logarithm.

2. This model is something of an oversimplification, not least in the assumption that the supply of jobs is sufficient to make whether or not an individual has a job a function of his or her own choice.

5. CAVEAT EMPTOR

In the preceding chapters, I have sought to provide an introduction to models for censored, sample-selected, and truncated data. There is little doubt that since the late 1970s, such models have come to be very widely used in the social science community. However, in recent years, it has gradually become evident that these techniques also can be problematic, and a good deal of criticism has been leveled at the Heckman model in particular. Although the jury is still out in many respects, it is now clear that these models need to be approached with a degree of care—hence, the title of this chapter, in which we look at three important issues in the practical application of models of censoring and sample selection. These are, first, their sensitivity to distributional assumptions; second, the question of the identification of the Heckman model; and finally, the utility of sample selection models in evaluation research. In all these areas we seek to present not only the problems associated with the methods but also suggestions of how to overcome them or of alternative methods that might be used. We conclude by providing a set of guidelines that will, we hope, allow users to avoid some possible pitfalls.

5.1 Sensitivity to Distributional Assumptions

5.1.1 Heteroscedasticity

Heteroscedasticity—or nonconstant variance of the error term—is a more important problem in censored and sample-selected models than in ordinary least squares. This is because least squares estimators are consistent, though not efficient, under heteroscedasticity, whereas censored and sample-selected estimators are neither consistent nor efficient (Amemiya, 1984, p. 23). The solution "is to make some reasonable assumption about the nature of the heteroscedasticity" (Maddala, 1983, p. 179).[1] In other words, decide on the functional form of the heteroscedasticity and write σ in the log-likelihood as a function of observed variables. Eliason (1993) shows how to do this in the case of a normally distributed error with heteroscedasticity (pp. 28-34) and for the truncated normal (pp. 63-66). Maddala (1983, p. 180) suggests that an "appealing" specification for the error term in a Tobit model is to set

$$\sigma_i = (\gamma + \delta z_i)^2.$$

Here, z can include some or all of the variables in the vector x and γ and δ are parameters to be estimated. To do this, we would simply replace σ in Equation 2.15 and in our definition of Φ_i with the above expression.

5.1.2 Nonnormality

Sample-selection bias methods themselves (as distinct from their specific implementations) may not make very stringent distributional assumptions (see Heckman & Robb, 1986, pp. 57-63). For example, Heckman's original two-step estimator requires only that (a) the error for the selection equation should be normal and (b) the conditional expectation of the outcome equation error, given the selection equation error, should be linear in the latter (Olsen, 1980, p. 1817). However, implementation using standard methods (two-stage or ML) also invokes assumptions about the distribution of the outcome equation error and/or the joint distribution of the two errors (e.g., bivariate normality).

Nonnormality in the context of censored and sample-selected models is potentially very damaging. Although OLS estimators are consistent under nonnormality, sample-selection and censored estimators are not. Goldberger (1983) examined a range of symmetric, but nonnormal, error distributions in the Tobit model and concluded that "the normal selection-bias adjustment procedure will be quite sensitive to modest departures from normality" (p. 79). More generally, Olsen (1982), writing of methods for correcting for selection bias, noted that "maximum likelihood methods have the little appreciated attribute that they are extremely sensitive to the assumption made about the population distribution of the regression residuals" (p. 236).

Given that nonnormality is potentially such a severe problem, how might we go about dealing with it? There are two broad approaches: If we have some grounds for assuming a known parametric distribution for the error(s), we can build this assumption into our model. Alternatively, if we are agnostic about the error distribution(s), we might employ semiparametric methods. We now discuss each of these approaches.

The most straightforward method for parametric estimation of models involving nonnormal errors is maximum likelihood, in which we specify the error distributions directly. Maddala (1983, pp. 187-190) gives two simple examples of nonnormal Tobit models. The first of these assumes that the error term, u, has a log-normal distribution. In this case, the model's log-likelihood is the same as usual except that we replace y with $\ln(y)$ and the censoring thresholds with their logged values. The second assumes that u has an exponential distribution, for which the density and distribution functions have very simple forms. The Tobit model is relatively easy to extend to nonnormal distributions because it involves only a univariate distribution. So, as Greene (1991, p. 588) has pointed out, accelerated failure time models, as used in survival analysis, are censored regression models, but they usually have a nonnormal error distribution. Typical distributions are Weibull, log-logistic, exponential, Gompertz, and so on (Allison, 1984). Thus, with little difficulty, software for these models can be employed to estimate nonnormal Tobits.

Matters are more complicated with ML sample-selection models proper, where we need to deal with the bivariate distribution of the error terms from the selection and outcome equations. An example of how this might be done is provided by Lee (1983). The original Heckman probit-OLS approach to sample selection bias requires normality of the selection equation error. However, Lee (1983), building on the earlier work of Olsen (1980), presents a very flexible two-stage approach that can be applied to models where this error is nonnormal (although we have to make some assumptions about how it is distributed). His method is quite simple: compute the selection model, based on whatever assumption for the error is valid; compute the predicted probabilities; find the inverse normal distribution function for these probabilities (i.e., what value of $\mathbf{w}_i'\alpha = j_i$ would, when inserted into $\Phi(.)$, yield the same probability as the predicted ones); then evaluate the normal density and distribution functions at j_i to compute the estimate of λ_i.

This can be very useful in the situation in which the selection equation involves more than two categories—so-called polychotomous selection models. For example, suppose we were looking at math performance among pupils in four types of school. We might specify this problem as a selection equation, involving the four alternative types of school ($m = 1$ . . . 4) with an outcome equation whose dependent variable (score in math test) is observed among pupils in each kind of school. Lee's approach might be implemented by using a multinomial logit for the choice of school: The predicted probabilities of entering each type of school for each pupil would be computed, and from them we would calculate j_{im}, $m = 1$ . . . 4. These quantities then would be used to compute corresponding estimates of λ_{im}, which could be employed in, say, four OLS regressions.[2]

Lee's (1983) method is more general than this, however, in that it allows for nonnormal (but known) distributions not only of the selection error, e, but also of the outcome equation error, u. In this case, the inverse normal distribution function can be used to transform e and u to normality and their joint distribution to bivariate normality; Lee (1983) and Maddala (1983, pp. 272-275) provide details. This allows us to use ML methods. We begin with the usual selection and outcome equations:

$$z_i^* = w_i'\alpha + e_i \qquad (5.1a)$$

$$z_i = 0 \text{ if } z_i^* \leq 0;$$

$$z_i = 1 \text{ if } z_i^* > 0$$

$$y_i^* = x_i'\beta + u_i \qquad (5.1b)$$

$$y_i = y_i^* \text{ if } z_i = 1$$

$$y_i = \text{not observed if } z_i = 0$$

and u and e are assumed to have correlation ρ. However, we now suppose that u has a distribution whose density is denoted by $g(u)$ and cumulative distribution function by $G(u)$, and e has a distribution whose cumulative distribution function we denote by $F(e)$. F and G may not be the normal distribution function. However, if we denote the inverse of the standard normal distribution function by Φ^{-1}, we can define a new variable, e^*, as

$$e^* = \Phi^{-1}[F(e)] .$$

This is the transformation we described verbally above: Find the value that, when inserted into the standard normal distribution function, yields the same probability as $F(e)$. We can apply the same transformation to u:

$$u^* = \Phi^{-1}[G(u)].$$

Both e^* and u^* will be distributed as standard normals. The bivariate distribution

$$B\{\Phi^{-1}[F(e)], \Phi^{-1}[G(u)], \rho\}$$

will, because of the normality of u^* and e^*, be bivariate normal. To estimate the model of Equations 5.1a and 5.1b using ML, we then simply substitute these expressions in the log-likelihood for the sample selection model shown in Equation 3.10, which yields

$$L = \sum_0 \log[1 - F(w_i'\alpha)] + \sum_1 \log\{g[(y_i - x_i'\beta)/\sigma_u]\} \qquad (5.2)$$

$$+ \sum_1 \log\Phi\left[\frac{\Phi^{-1}[F(w_i'\alpha)] + \rho\{\Phi^{-1}[G(y_i - x_i'\beta)/\sigma_u]\}}{(1-\rho^2)^{1/2}}\right].$$

Here, $F(\mathbf{w}_i'\alpha)$ is the probability that e is less than $\mathbf{w}_i'\alpha$, and $G[(y_i - \mathbf{x}_i'\beta)/\sigma_u)$ is the probability that u is less than $(y_i - \mathbf{x}_i'\beta)/\sigma_u$. Φ^{-1} in the last part of the log-likelihood indicates the calculation of the values of a standard, normally distributed variable that would give rise to the same probabilities when inserted into the function $\Phi(.)$. Note that if e and u are normal, then this reduces to Equation 3.10 because g would be the normal density function, F would be the same as Φ, and Φ^{-1} would cancel with both F and G in the last line of Equation 5.2. In practice, this is a very flexible method of transforming nonnormally distributed errors into a form that can be used in the usual (two-step or ML) methods of estimation for censored and sample-selected data (although in some cases, it will be necessary to introduce additional restrictions to ensure that the model produces estimates of the error terms that fall within the permissible range of the particular distributions that have been chosen).

If we have no information as to how the relevant error terms are distributed, we might use a semiparametric method. Recall that the Heckman method requires that we estimate the vector α from the selection equation and use this to find an expression for

$$E(outcome\ error|selection\ error > w_i'\alpha).$$

Newey, Powell, and Walker (1990) describe and illustrate two semiparametric methods of estimating α and two semiparametric methods of estimating the β coefficients in the outcome equation given estimates of α. However, as Maddala (1992, p. 56) has noted, these semiparametric approaches are still in their early stages, and empirical applications are rare. Furthermore, the derivation of these estimators is beyond the level of this text: Interested readers should consult the papers by Newey et al. (1990); Coslett (1991), which provides a semiparametric estimator for the sample selection model; and Powell (1984), which presents a semiparametric Tobit model. Lee (1994) presents a more general semiparametric approach to handling censored and sample-selected regression problems.[3]

Given the sensitivity of the usual estimators for these models to deviations from normality and homoscedasticity, it is obviously valuable to be able to test these assumptions. Several approaches have been suggested (e.g., Lee & Maddala, 1985). Some of the tests for deviations from normality and homoscedasticity are tests against one or more specific alternatives. However, one particularly useful set of tests is advanced by Chesher and Irish (1987). These permit, among other things, tests for homoscedasticity and normality that do not require specific alternative formulations of either heteroscedasticity or a nonnormal distribution. Their test for normality, for example, generalizes standard tests for normality based on skewness and kurtosis to the case of censored sample models where the standardized residuals on which the test is based are not directly observable because the latent dependent variable is itself only partially observed.

Readers interested in the details of the Chesher and Irish tests should consult their article. The underlying idea is to test the moments of the estimated distribution of the standardized (mean zero and standard deviation of one) residuals from the regression of the latent variable, y^*, against what they should be if the assumption of normality is correct—that is, the corresponding moments of the standard normal distribution. The test involves three main steps: first, calculating the standardized residuals, given that y^* is only partially observed; second, computing the differences between the moments of these residuals and those of the normal distribution (these quantities are called "moment residuals," and the tests involve a maximum of the first four moments—mean, variance, skewness, and kurtosis); and third, calculating a "score test" to assess the significance of the latter differences—or, more formally, to test the null hypothesis that the observed distribution of the residuals does not differ significantly from what would be expected if their true distribution were normal. A similar approach underlies their test for homoscedasticity.

Their tests are easy to compute because they can be reduced to a simple regression. In the test for homoscedasticity, it is necessary to compute the first two "moment residuals"; in the test for normality, the first four. This is easy because they involve only functions of the observed y, the explanatory variables, and the estimated β and σ (I show how these are computed for the Tobit in Appendix B). These moment residuals are then used, together with the explanatory variables, to form a new matrix **R**. A vector of ones is regressed on this matrix, and the resulting explained sum of squares is then used to test the null hypothesis (of either homoscedasticity or normality). This is done using a simple chi-squared test. The method is explained in more detail in Appendix B. Similar approaches to testing for normality can be found in Bera, Jarque, and Lee (1984) and Davidson and MacKinnon (1984).

5.2 Identification and Robustness

A number of authors (e.g., Little, 1985) have expressed misgivings about the use of nonlinearity to achieve identification in the original probit-OLS approach to correcting for sample selection bias. As Berk and Ray (1982) note, a number of problems can arise from this:

> High variance estimates typically result. It is also quite common to find substantial multicollinearity between the hazard rate instrument and the other regressors in the substantive [outcome] equation. . . . Finally, if one is unable to explain much of the variation in the selection process . . . the hazard rate [inverse Mill's ratio] instrument will have very little variance . . . [leading to] . . . high collinearity with the intercept in the substantive equation. (p. 386)

An example of such multicollinearity is provided by Duan, Manning, Morris, and Newhouse (1984, p. 288), who find a multiple squared correlation, R^2, between the inverse Mill's ratio and the other explanatory variables in their outcome (or, as Berk and Ray term it, *substantive*) equation in excess of 0.8 in all nine of their samples. Recall, too, that in our discussion of Hagan and Parker (1985), we noted that the standard error of the inverse Mill's ratio's coefficient in their outcome equation was almost equal in size to the coefficient itself, and that the clearest effect of its inclusion was to reduce the constant term to around two thirds of its uncorrected value.

Stolzenberg and Relles (1990), in a widely cited Monte Carlo study, find very unpromising results for the Heckman two-step method even when bivariate normality of selection and outcome errors is maintained. Using samples of 500 and severe (90%) censoring, they find that, in their simulations, Heckman's method performed, on average, no better than OLS in terms of the bias and accuracy of the relevant parameter estimates. This leads them to conclude that Heckman's method should play a "small and infrequent" role in assessing and correcting sample-selection bias.

The Stolzenberg and Relles article has been seen as sounding a severe warning to the social science community about the dangers of the Heckman approach for correcting sample-selection bias (e.g., see Land & McCall,

1993). However, Stolzenberg and Relles's results are wholly consistent with an earlier Monte Carlo study by Nelson (1984), whose interpretation suggests that the situations in which the Heckman two-step technique is likely to prove questionable can be identified easily.

The issue that underlies Nelson's article is a comparison of the performance of OLS, the Heckman two-step method, and ML in correcting for sample-selection bias, given the usual setup of a selection and an outcome equation. In particular, he focuses on the relative efficiency of each method (i.e., the variances of the parameter estimates), and thus he also addresses the concerns voiced by Berk and Ray (1982) and many others. Given bivariate normality of errors, there are three important factors influencing the performance of the Heckman estimator:

1. The correlation, ρ, between the error terms, u and e, of the outcome and selection equations
2. The correlation between the sets of explanatory variables, x and w, in each equation
3. The degree of censoring or sample selection (i.e., the proportion of cases for which $z = 1$)

In both the Nelson and the Stolzenberg and Relles studies, the third factor is taken as fixed, and the other two are varied over the different simulations. In the latter study, the use of very severe sample selection (with only 10% of the sample selected) favors OLS over the two-step approach because it makes the latter estimator very inefficient, all other things equal. This is because the efficiency of the two-step approach will depend upon the extent to which the estimate of the inverse Mill's ratio, λ_i, which is used to correct for selection bias, is correlated with the other explanatory variables in the outcome equation. As in the study by Duan et al. (1984), this can be measured by R^2, the coefficient of determination from the regression of the estimated λ_i on the x_i variables. The size of this R^2 will depend on Factor 2 and, given this, on the degree of censoring or sample selection, Factor 3.

To see this, suppose that x and w are identical, and we are therefore relying on the nonlinearity of the probit for identification in the outcome equation. The estimate of λ_i is a nonlinear function of these variables: But if the range of these variables is limited (as it is when censoring or sample selection is severe), a linear function of them becomes an increasingly good approximation to the nonlinear λ_i. Put another way, the Mill's ratio instrument becomes an increasingly linear function of the variables of which it is made up as sample selection becomes more severe. So, R^2 will increase for a given correlation between x and w as sample selection becomes more extreme. This will worsen the efficiency of the two-step method (and of ML) relative to OLS (which does not use the estimated Mill's ratio).

In Chapter 3, we saw that OLS estimates will be unbiased if either of two conditions are met: (a) if the error correlation, ρ, is zero; or (b) if the estimate of λ_i is uncorrelated with the explanatory variables in the outcome equation (that is, $R^2 = 0$).

If neither of these conditions is met, then an increasingly nonzero ρ or an increase in R^2 (which, as we have seen, depends upon Factors 2 and 3) will lead to increasing bias in the OLS coefficients (Nelson, 1984, p. 193). Thus, the need to correct for sample selection becomes greater. But, as we have already seen, any nonzero R^2 will lead to a loss of efficiency in the two-step (and also ML) estimators relative to OLS. Thus, in broad terms, there is a trade-off: The two-step estimator is consistent in circumstances where OLS is not, but the variances of the parameter estimates are likely to be much greater. This also suggests that the use of the two-step method to estimate the Tobit model should be handled with extreme caution, given that here the explanatory variables in each equation are the same. The greater variance of the two-step Tobit estimates relative to both OLS and ML is evident in Table 2.2.

But the focus of Stolzenberg and Relles (1990) was the accuracy and bias of the OLS and two-step estimators rather than their efficiency. Given $\rho \neq 0$ and $R^2 \neq 0$, neither estimator will be unbiased, although the latter will be consistent. Consistency is a large-sample property. However, Stolzenberg and Relles used a sample of 500 in each of their simulations, and, given 90% censoring (or nonselection), their outcome equation therefore must have been estimated using only 50 cases. Under these conditions, we should probably not expect the two-step estimator to be particularly accurate. Despite this, Table 4 of Stolzenberg and Relles shows that whenever either or both of ρ and the correlation between their single x and single w variables exceeds 0.5, the bias of the two-step estimator is less than that of OLS. With a larger sample or less severe censoring, the relative difference in performance would be even more marked.

The efficiency of the two-step and ML estimators is least when ρ is low and R^2 is high. Overall, the ML estimators of both β and ρ are much more efficient than the two-step estimators. And, in particular, "the conditions under which the OLS bias is largest are precisely the conditions under which the dominance of the MLE over the two-step estimator is greatest" (Nelson, 1984, p. 195). In general, although ML gives rise to larger variance estimates than does OLS, the differences (except where R^2 is very high indeed—say > 0.9) are minor. Thus, whenever OLS is biased (and also inconsistent), ML is to be preferred to both OLS and the two-step approach.

5.3 Sample-Selection Models in Evaluation Research

One area in which sample selection models have been much criticized is in their application in the evaluation of labor market programs (Fraker & Maynard, 1987; Lalonde, 1986). This arose because, in the few cases where random assignment was used in such programs, nonexperimental estimators for overcoming sample-selection bias did not seem to estimate the "true" (or, more accurately, random assignment-based measures of) program effects accurately. This led, in turn, to calls for randomized clinical trials to be used to evaluate such programs (Ashenfelter & Card, 1985; Barnow, 1987). In a number of articles, Heckman has argued that these conclusions about the limitations of nonexperimental methods are based on misapplications of methods for correcting selection bias: They have either been inappropriate given the nature of the samples used, or they have incorporated unnecessary and overly restrictive assumptions. In reanalyses, Heckman, Hotz, and Dabos (1987) and Heckman and Hotz (1989) have demonstrated that some nonexperimental methods do indeed give results very close to those that would be arrived at by random assignment.

From the point of view of this exposition, this debate draws attention to two related features: first, that methods for controlling for selection bias in evaluation research and elsewhere are by no means exhausted by those presented so far (e.g., see Heckman & Robb, 1986; Little & Rubin, 1987), and second, the methods that are appropriate depend on the data available and the social processes that underlie the phenomena under investigation (e.g., how trainees are selected into a particular program). I will give two examples.

Imagine that we want to assess the effectiveness of two types of school, A and B, in terms of examination performance among their students. If we have data on students from a single cross-section, then the normal ML estimation of the selection (which school type a student attends) and outcome (exam performance conditional on attending a given type of school) stages is an obvious route to follow. But suppose we have data—including examination results—from this sample for two points in time—before they entered their respective schools and after spending some time in either school type A or B. One approach to correcting for selection bias is to write the performance of the ith pupil in the tth ($t = 1, 2$) exam as

$$y_{it} = \beta x_{it} + \gamma z_i + u_{it} \text{ and } u_{it} = \xi_i + \nu_{it} \, .$$

The selection equation for which school a student attends is

$$z_i = \alpha w_i + e_i \text{ and } e_i = \xi_i + \varepsilon_i \, .$$

Here, $z = 1$ if the student attends school type A, $z = 0$ if school type B, and $z = 0$ for all students at $t = 1$. Sample selection arises because of the correlation between u and e induced by the common factor ξ. We assume that ν_{it} has a zero mean and constant variance, and that it is independent of ε and of all other values of $\nu_{it'}(t' \neq t)$. The correlation between e and u then can be removed by taking the first difference of the outcome equations:

$$y_{i2} - y_{i1} = \beta(x_{i2} - x_{i1}) + \gamma z_i + u_{i2} - u_{i1}$$

$$= \beta(x_{i2} - x_{i1}) + \gamma z_i + (\nu_{i2} - \nu_{i1}) \, .$$

The error term in this equation is then independent of the other explanatory variables and has a constant variance and zero mean. Therefore, we can use OLS to regress the difference between the later and earlier exam scores on the change in the values of the explanatory variables between the two points in time and the dummy variable for type of school. Note that γ—the effect of being in one school type rather than the other—is identified in this equation. Intuitively, we can view ξ as an omitted, student-specific, time-invariant factor that influences both choice of school and exam performance. By taking the difference or change in exam performance over time, this factor drops out. Heckman and Hotz (1989) present elaborations of this model depending on the number of time points for which one has observations.

A second alternative approach, this time applicable to cross-sectional data of the kind we have been dealing with throughout this monograph, is Rubin's (1977) mixture modeling method (see Land & McCall, 1993, for an introduction). Rubin introduced this method in the context of imputing values of a dependent variable in the presence of nonresponse to surveys, but because nonresponse is a variety of sample-selection problem, this method could, in principle, be applied more widely. Rubin adopts a Bayesian approach in which the investigator computes the likely degree of bias in estimating the outcome variable, conditional on his or her prior belief about the relationship between the parameters of the distribution of the dependent variable among the respondent (selected) and nonrespondent (nonselected) subsamples. In other words, the investigator first makes a guess at, or assumption about, the distribution of the dependent variable in the nonselected part of the sample; together with knowledge of the dependent variable in the selected sample, this implies something about the distribution of the dependent variable in the entire sample. The method then permits the investigator to assess the sensitivity of the resulting distribution of the dependent variable in the whole sample to the assumptions made about how this variable is distributed in the nonselected part of the sample. As Land and McCall (1993, pp. 302-303) make clear, the contrast with selection bias methods is that whereas these require that we hypothesize and fit a model of the selection process, the mixture modeling approach requires an assumption about the unobserved distribution of the dependent variable.

These assumptions are formalized in the mixture modeling approach, and information from the existence of fully observed explanatory variables can be used in shaping these assumptions. A predictive Bayesian probability interval (akin to a confidence interval) can be computed for a given assumption; typically, however, such an interval will be wide in relation to the more usual confidence intervals. It is also quite likely that the "prior" on which the assumption is based will not be well defined: In the examples given by Land and McCall, it is assumed that the mean of the dependent variable for the nonrespondents is the same as for the respondents, but the variance is assumed to be larger. One can see, then, that this procedure could be of considerable value if one had strong prior knowledge that could be brought to bear in forming one's assumptions, or if the results proved to be very insensitive to various assumptions. But a serious difficulty would arise if, as is likely, one did not have any strong priors and the results were sensitive to one's assumptions. This suggests that the method may be most useful in telling us how much of a problem nonresponse or selection bias seems to be rather than in correcting for it.

5.4 Some Guidelines for the Use of Censored and Sample-Selection Models

In conclusion, I provide a rough guide to the careful use of models for censoring and sample selection. The first issue concerns which method of dealing with censoring or selection bias is most appropriate. If the data are to be collected, then this should be done with a view to minimizing sample-selection problems. For example, in the case of an evaluation, it may be possible to use a research design involving random allocation of participants to control and treatment groups. If the data are already collected, then we need to choose the most appropriate methods among those that the data will allow. So, if longitudinal data are available, it will be possible to use methods such as those presented by Heckman and Hotz (1989) and discussed above. If the data are cross-sectional, then we will probably have to use the kinds of methods presented in Chapters 2 through 4.

An important issue is sample size. All of the desirable properties of the various estimators discussed in this monograph relate to large samples. Therefore, if one's sample is small, one may have to accept that it is simply too small to permit the use of these methods. In turn, this suggests that if the substantive questions driving research can be answered only using the methods we have discussed, the research design must ensure that a suitably large sample is available.

Given a suitably large sample, and assuming that we are going to use the methods presented in this monograph, the first step is to test for homoscedasticity and normality. This can be done using the Chesher and Irish (1987) approach or one of a number of similar alternatives (Bera et al., 1984; Davidson & MacKinnon, 1984). Chesher and Irish explain fully how to test for homoscedasticity and normality in the Tobit case; this could be extended to the sample-selection model, but here we would be testing bivariate normality, so this extension would be more complex. But in the case of sample-selection models, we can use their approach to test for normality for each step—selection and outcome—separately. It is particularly important to test for normality in the selection equation. This can be done most easily by estimating this equation separately as a probit and applying the Chesher and Irish tests.

If the assumption of homoscedasticity is not met, then it will be necessary to hypothesize a functional form for the variance. Similarly, if the error distribution(s) are not normal, it will be necessary to either choose another distribution or use a semiparametric approach. If these assumptions are met, however, then for the censored regression model, the Tobit estimates should be accepted. For the sample-selection model, however, one should first compute the inverse Mill's ratio instrument using a probit and regress this on the explanatory (x) variables that appear in the outcome equation. If the R^2 from this regression is around zero, then the outcome equation can be estimated using uncorrected OLS. If this is not so, then the two stages of the model should be estimated using ML. If, however, the estimate of ρ in the ML model is around zero, it is advisable once again to estimate the outcome equation as an uncorrected OLS regression. This is because the OLS estimates of β will differ little, if at all, from the ML estimates, but they will have smaller variances (particularly if R^2 is large). In summary, when estimating the sample-selection model, use an uncorrected OLS for the outcome equation if either R^2 or the estimate of ρ is near zero; otherwise, use ML. Given the availability of ML methods, there is little to be said in favor of using the original two-step approach.

A final point: When is it appropriate to use the censored regression (Tobit) model rather than the sample selection model? This question has been raised by Maddala (1992, p. 54), who suggests that the Tobit has been inappropriate for virtually all applications in which it has been used—including the original application by Tobin (1958). His argument is that the bunching of y values at some limit is not in itself sufficient justification for the use of the model; rather, we should ask why this bunching occurs. If it is because of some decision on the part of the individuals we are studying (such as a decision not to spend any money on luxury goods), then the censored regression model is not appropriate. What is needed here is explicit modeling of the decision followed by modeling of the dependent variable conditional upon this decision having been made—in other words, a sample-selection model. On the other hand, if the bunching of the y values occurs because of some exogenous mechanism—such as the way in which data were collected or recorded (as in the example of examination scores with which we began)—the censored regression model is unproblematically appropriate.

Whether one should use the censored or sample-selection model when the observability of y^* is a function of individuals' decisions depends on the nature and interpretation of the latent variable, y^*. For example, suppose that y^* is taken to be desired years of education. We presume that for those young people who remain in education after the minimum school-leaving age, observed years of education, y, are equal to desired years, but for those who leave at the minimum age, desired years are less than or equal to this minimum value. In this case, if we are interested in modeling desired years of education, it is not sensible to model the decision of whether or not to remain in education beyond the minimum age as a decision distinct from the desired years of education. Thus, the censored regression model is appropriate. On the other hand, we could not sensibly argue that the latent variable in the expenditure on luxury goods model could be interpreted as "desired expenditure" because this would allow negative desired expenditures. In this case, then, Maddala may well be correct in arguing that the decision to spend at least something should be modeled separately from the amount spent. When we should use one or the other model is not a question of methodology; rather, it is a question of interpretation and theoretical plausibility.

5.5 Concluding Remarks

This monograph has introduced the commonly used techniques for regression analysis when the dependent variable is censored, sample selected, or truncated. We have also sought to show the links between these and other models and to illustrate how the basic approach can be extended in several ways. We have, however, ended on a note of caution. Many of the desirable properties of the estimators discussed here hold only for large samples, and these models are much less robust than are ordinary regression models to violations of the assumptions of homoscedasticity and normality. Nevertheless, problems of sample selection and censoring are pervasive in the social sciences. This is testified to by the number of social science articles that have used one or another of the techniques presented here. Although these techniques need to be used with care, they provide a valuable and powerful means of dealing with these pervasive problems.

Notes

1. Of course, it is important to emphasize that here we are talking about heteroscedasticity in the error term of the latent variable, y^*. It is important to distinguish this from the heteroscedasticity that arises in the outcome equation of the Heckman two-step method, to which we referred in Chapter 3.

2. The log-likelihood function also can be constructed for this case, following a generalization of the approach described later in this chapter. The robustness of Lee's approach when applied to polychotomous selection models has been questioned by Schmertmann (1994), although his criticisms do not apply when the Lee method is employed in the usual dichotomous selection equation setup.

3. A number of the papers in the *Journal of Econometrics,* Annals 1986-1 on "Continuous and Discrete Econometric Models With Unspecified Error Distributions," edited by Greg Duncan, also deal with censored regression models.

APPENDIX A: THE EXPECTED VALUE
OF A TRUNCATED NORMAL VARIABLE

This appendix presents the standard results for the expected value of a truncated, normally distributed random variable. Let u be a normally distributed random variable with mean zero and standard deviation σ. The expected values of u when it is truncated at the value m are as follows:

A.1 Truncation From Above

The probability that $u \leq m$ is

$$\Phi\left(\frac{m}{\sigma}\right) = \int_{-\infty}^{m/\sigma} \frac{1}{\sqrt{2\pi}} \exp(-t^2/2)dt \,,$$

and the expected value of u conditional on $u \leq m$, $E(u \mid u \leq m)$, is

$$\frac{\phi(m/\sigma)}{\Phi(m/\sigma)} \,. \tag{A1}$$

A.2 Truncation From Below

The probability that $u > m$ is

$$\int_{m/\sigma}^{\infty} \frac{1}{\sqrt{2\pi}} \exp(-t^2/2)dt = 1 - \Phi(m/\sigma),$$

and the expected value of u conditional on $u > m$, $E(u \mid u > m)$, is

$$\frac{\phi(m/\sigma)}{1 - \Phi(m/\sigma)} \,. \tag{A2}$$

Confusion is sometimes caused by virtue of the fact that Equations A1 and A2 can be written in other ways that make use of the symmetry of the normal distribution. From our point of view, this symmetry implies two things. First, $1 - \Phi(m/\sigma) = \Phi(-m/\sigma)$; and second, $\phi(m/\sigma) = \phi(-m/\sigma)$. So,

74

for example, if we define $m = c - x_i'\beta$, then we can write, for example, $E(u \mid u > c - x_i'\beta)$ as

$$\frac{\phi\left(\dfrac{c - x_i'\beta}{\sigma}\right)}{\Phi\left(\dfrac{x_i'\beta - c}{\sigma}\right)} = \frac{\phi\left(\dfrac{x_i'\beta - c}{\sigma}\right)}{\Phi\left(\dfrac{x_i'\beta - c}{\sigma}\right)}.$$

The latter is the expression we used in our exposition of the Tobit model. Equally, $E(u \mid u \le c - x_i'\beta)$ can be written in a variety of ways:

$$\frac{-\phi\left(\dfrac{c - x_i'\beta}{\sigma}\right)}{\Phi\left(\dfrac{c - x_i'\beta}{\sigma}\right)} = \frac{-\phi\left(\dfrac{x_i'\beta - c}{\sigma}\right)}{\Phi\left(\dfrac{c - x_i'\beta}{\sigma}\right)} = \frac{-\phi\left(\dfrac{x_i'\beta - c}{\sigma}\right)}{1 - \Phi\left(\dfrac{x_i'\beta - c}{\sigma}\right)}.$$

APPENDIX B: CHESHER AND IRISH'S TESTS FOR NORMALITY AND HOMOSCEDASTICITY

To implement Chesher and Irish's (1987) tests requires the computation of estimates of the first four "moment residuals," $\hat{e}^{(m)}$, $m = 1$ to 4. Let z_i be the censoring indicator ($z_i = 0$ for censored observations) and define $k_i = x_i'\beta/\sigma$ and $\lambda(k_i)$ as the inverse Mill's ratio evaluated at k_i. Then the first four moment residuals in the Tobit case are

$$\hat{e}^{(1)} = -(1 - z_i)\lambda(k_i) + z_i\left(\frac{y}{\sigma} - k_i\right)$$

$$\hat{e}^{(2)} = (1 - z_i)k_i\lambda(k_i) + z_i\left[\left(\frac{y}{\sigma} - k_i\right)^2 - 1\right]$$

$$\hat{e}^{(3)} = -(1 - z_i)(2 + k_i^2)\lambda(k_i) + z_i\left(\frac{y}{\sigma} - k_i\right)^3$$

$$\hat{e}^{(4)} = (1 - z_i)(3k_i + k_i^3)\lambda(k_i) + z_i\left[\left(\frac{y}{\sigma} - k_i\right)^4 - 3\right]$$

In practice, we use the estimated values of β and σ in forming these quantities.

In the test for normality, the elements of the matrix $\mathbf{R}$ are

$$\hat{e}^{(1)}x, \hat{e}^{(2)}, \hat{e}^{(3)}, \hat{e}^{(4)}.$$

If $\mathbf{x}$ includes a constant term, $\hat{e}^{(2)}$ can be omitted. In practice, then, to test for normality in the Tobit using the Chesher and Irish method, we would compute, for each observation, the quantities $\hat{e}^{(m)}$ and then take each of the x_k, $k = 1, \ldots K$ variables in our model (including the constant term) and multiply its value by $\hat{e}^{(1)}$ to form a new set of variables. In total, we would then have a matrix $\mathbf{R}$ with $K + 2$ columns. We next regress a vector of ones on $\mathbf{R}$ and compute the explained sum of squares. This yields the Lagrange Multiplier (LM) statistic, which has a chi-squared distribution with, in this case, two degrees of freedom. Thus, if the value of the LM statistic exceeds the critical value for chi-squared with 2 *df*, we must reject the null hypothesis of normality.

The test for heteroscedasticity works in a very similar fashion. Chesher and Irish (1987, p. 41) also show the elements of $\mathbf{R}$ for the probit model. This is particularly useful for our purposes, insofar as it provides a test for the normality of the selection equation in sample-selection models. A word of caution: This LM test is not believed to have good small sample properties and thus is to be relied upon only when the sample is relatively large.

REFERENCES

ACHEN, C. H. (1982) *Interpreting and Using Regression.* Sage University Paper series on Quantitative Applications in the Social Sciences, 07-029. Beverly Hills, CA: Sage.

ALDRICH, J. H., and NELSON, F. D. (1984) *Linear Probability, Logit and Probit Models.* Sage University Paper series on Quantitative Applications in the Social Sciences, 07-045. Beverly Hills, CA: Sage.

ALLISON, P. D. (1984) *Event History Analysis.* Sage University Paper series on Quantitative Applications in the Social Sciences, 07-046. Beverly Hills, CA: Sage.

ALLISON, P. D., and LONG, J. S. (1987) "Interuniversity mobility of academic scientists." *American Sociological Review* 52: 643-652.

AMEMIYA, T. (1979) "The estimation of simultaneous-equation Tobit model." *International Economic Review* 20: 169-181.

AMEMIYA, T. (1984) "Tobit models: A survey." *Journal of Econometrics* 24: 3-61.

ASHENFELTER, O., and CARD, D. (1985) "Using the longitudinal structure of earnings to estimate the effect of training programs." *Review of Economics and Statistics* 67: 648-660.

BARNOW, B. S. (1987) "The impact of CETA programs on earnings: A review of the literature." *Journal of Human Resources* 22: 157-193.

BARNOW, B. S., CAIN, G. G., and GOLDBERGER, A. S. (1980) "Issues in the analysis of selectivity bias." In E. W. Stromsdorfer & G. Farkas (Eds.), *Evaluation Studies Review Annual* (Vol. 5, pp. 43-59). Beverly Hills, CA: Sage.

BERA, A. K., JARQUE, C. M., and LEE, L. F. (1984) "Testing the normality assumption in limited dependent variable models." *International Economic Review* 25: 563-578.

BERK, R. A. (1983) "An introduction to sample selection bias in sociological data." *American Sociological Review* 48: 386-398.

BERK, R. A., and RAY, S. C. (1982) "Selection biases in sociological data." *Social Science Research* 11: 352-398.

CHESHER, A., and IRISH, M. (1987) "Residual analysis in the grouped and censored normal linear model." *Journal of Econometrics* 34: 33-61.

COLEMAN, J. S., HOFFER, T., and KILGORE, S. (1982) *High School Achievement: Public, Catholic and Other Private Schools Compared.* New York: Basic Books.

CRAGG, J. (1971) "Some statistical models for limited dependent variables with applications to the demand for durable goods." *Econometrica* 39: 829-844.

DAVIDSON, R., and MACKINNON, J. G. (1984) "Convenient specification tests for logit and probit models." *Journal of Econometrics* 25: 241-262.

DEEGAN, J., Jr., and WHITE, K. J. (1976) "An analysis of nonpartisan election media expenditure decisions using limited dependent variable methods." *Social Science Research* 5: 127-135.

DHRYMES, P. (1989) *Topics in Advanced Econometrics.* New York: Springer-Verlag.

DUAN, N., MANNING, W. G., MORRIS, C. N., and NEWHOUSE, J. P. (1984) "Choosing between the sample-selection model and the multi-part model." *Journal of Business and Economic Statistics* 2: 283-289.

77

ELIASON, S. R. (1993) *Maximum Likelihood Estimation: Logic and Practice*. Sage University Paper series on Quantitative Applications in the Social Sciences, 07-096. Newbury Park, CA: Sage.

ENGLAND, P., FARKAS, G., KILBOURNE, B. S., and DOU, T. (1988) "Explaining occupational sex segregation and wages: Findings from a model with fixed effects." *American Sociological Review* 53: 544-558.

FIN, T., and SCHMIDT, P. (1984) "A test of the Tobit specification against an alternative suggested by Cragg." *Review of Economics and Statistics* 66: 174-177.

FRAKER, T., and MAYNARD, R. (1987) "Evaluating comparison group designs with employment-related programs." *Journal of Human Resources* 22: 194-227.

GOLDBERGER, A. S. (1981) "Linear regression after selection." *Journal of Econometrics* 15: 357-366.

GOLDBERGER, A. S. (1983) "Abnormal selection bias." In S. Karlin, T. Amemiya, & L. A. Goodman (Eds.), *Studies in Econometrics, Time Series and Multivariate Statistics* (pp. 67-84). New York: Academic Press.

GREENE, W. H. (1981) "Sample selection bias as a specification error: A comment." *Econometrica* 49: 795-798.

GREENE, W. H. (1990) *Econometric Analysis*. New York: Macmillan.

GREENE, W. H. (1991) *LIMDEP User's Manual and Reference Guide, Version 6.0*. New York: Econometric Software.

GRONAU, R. (1974) "Wage comparisons—A selectivity bias." *Journal of Political Economy* 82: 1119-1143.

HAGAN, J. (1989) *Structural Criminology*. New Brunswick, NJ: Rutgers University Press.

HAGAN, J., and PARKER, P. (1985) "White collar crime and punishment: The class structure and legal sanctioning of securities violations." *American Sociological Review* 50: 302-316.

HAUSMAN, J. A., and WISE, D. A. (1977) "Social experimentation, truncated distributions and efficient estimation." *Econometrica* 45: 919-939.

HECKMAN, J. J. (1974) "Shadow prices, market wages and labour supply." *Econometrica* 42: 679-694.

HECKMAN, J. J. (1976) "The common structure of statistical models of truncation, sample selection and limited dependent variables and a simple estimator for such models." *Annals of Economic and Social Measurement* 5: 475-492.

HECKMAN, J. J. (1979) "Sample selection bias as a specification error." *Econometrica* 47: 153-161.

HECKMAN, J. J. (1992) "Selection bias and self-selection." In J. Eatwell, M. Milgate, & P. Newman (Eds.), *The New Palgrave Econometrics* (pp. 201-224). London: Macmillan.

HECKMAN, J. J., and HOTZ, V. J. (1989) "Choosing among alternative nonexperimental methods for estimating the impact of social programs: The case of manpower training." *Journal of the American Statistical Association* 84(408): 862-874.

HECKMAN, J. J., HOTZ, V. J., and DABOS, M. (1987) "Do we need experimental data to evaluate the impact of manpower training on earnings?" *Evaluation Review* 11: 395-427.

HECKMAN, J. J., and ROBB, R. (1986) "Alternative identifying assumptions in econometric models of selection bias." *Advances in Econometrics* 5: 243-287.

HONOHAN, P., and NOLAN, B. (1993) *The Financial Assets of Households in Ireland*. Dublin: The Economic and Social Research Institute, General Research Series Paper 162.

JOHNSTON, J. (1972) *Econometric Methods* (2nd ed.). Tokyo: McGraw-Hill.

KALBFLEISCH, J. D., and PRENTICE, R. L. (1980) *The Statistical Analysis of Failure Time Data.* New York: John Wiley.

KARLIN, S., and TAYLOR, H. M. (1975) *A First Course in Stochastic Processes, Volume 1* (2nd ed.). New York: Academic Press.

KMENTA, J. (1971) *Elements of Econometrics.* New York: Macmillan.

LALONDE, R. (1986) "Evaluating the econometric evaluations of training programs with experimental data." *American Economic Review* 76: 604-620.

LAND, K. C., and MCCALL, P. L. (1993) "Estimating the effect of nonignorable nonresponse in sample surveys." *Sociological Methods & Research* 21: 291-316.

LEE, L. F. (1983) "Generalized econometric models with selectivity." *Econometrica* 51: 507-512.

LEE, L. F. (1994) "Semiparametric two stage estimation of sample selection models subject to Tobit-type selection rules." *Journal of Econometrics* 61: 305-344.

LEE, L. F., and MADDALA, G. S. (1985) "The common structure of tests for selectivity bias, serial correlation, heteroscedasticity and non-normality in the Tobit model." *International Economic Review* 26: 1-20.

LEWIS, H. G. (1974) "Comments on selectivity bias in wage comparisons." *Journal of Political Economy* 82: 1145-1156.

LEWIS-BECK, M. S. (1980) *Applied Regression: An Introduction.* Sage University Paper series on Quantitative Applications in the Social Sciences, 07-022. Beverly Hills, CA: Sage.

LITTLE, R. J. (1985) "A note about models for selectivity bias." *Econometrica* 53: 1469-1474.

LITTLE, R. J., and RUBIN, D. B. (1987) *Statistical Analysis With Missing Data.* New York: John Wiley.

MADDALA, G. S. (1983) *Limited Dependent and Qualitative Variables in Econometrics.* Cambridge: Cambridge University Press.

MADDALA, G. S. (1992) "Censored data models." In J. Eatwell, M. Milgate, & P. Newman (Eds.), *The New Palgrave Econometrics* (pp. 54-57). London: Macmillan.

MCDONALD, J. F., and MOFFIT, R. F. (1980) "The uses of Tobit analysis." *Review of Economics and Statistics* 62: 318-321.

MCKELVEY, R. D., and ZAVOINA, W. (1976) "A statistical model for the analysis of ordinal level dependent variables." *Journal of Mathematical Sociology* 4: 103-120.

NELSON, F. D. (1984) "Efficiency of the two-step estimator for models with endogenous sample selection." *Journal of Econometrics* 24: 181-196.

NEWEY, W. K., POWELL, J. L., and WALKER, J. R. (1990) "Semiparametric estimation of selection models: Some empirical results." *American Economic Review, AEA Papers and Proceedings* 80: 324-328.

OLSEN, R. J. (1978) "Comment on the uniqueness of the maximum likelihood estimator for the Tobit model." *Econometrica* 46: 1211-1215.

OLSEN, R. J. (1980) "A least squares correction for selectivity bias." *Econometrica* 48: 1815-1820.

OLSEN, R. J. (1982) "Distributional tests for selectivity bias and a more robust likelihood estimator." *International Economic Review* 23: 223-240.

PETERSON, R., and HAGAN, J. (1984) "Changing conceptions of race: Towards an account of anomalous findings of sentencing research." *American Sociological Review* 49: 56-70.

POWELL, J. L. (1984) "Least absolute deviations estimation for the censored regression model." *Journal of Econometrics* 25: 303-325.

RUBIN, D. B. (1977) "Formalizing subjective notions about the effect of nonrespondents in sample surveys." *Journal of the American Statistical Association* 72(359): 538-543.

SANDERS, J. M., and NEE, V. (1987) "Limits of ethnic solidarity in the enclave economy." *American Sociological Review* 52: 745-773.

SCHMERTMANN, C. P. (1994) "Selectivity bias correction methods in polychotomous sample selection models." *Journal of Econometrics* 35: 101-132.

STEWART, M. (1983) "On least-squares estimation when the dependent variable is grouped." *Review of Economic Studies* 50: 141-149.

STOLZENBERG, R. M., and RELLES, D. A. (1990) "Theory testing in a world of constrained research design." *Sociological Methods & Research* 18: 395-415.

TIENDA, M., SMITH, S. A., and ORTIZ, V. (1987) "Industrial restructuring, gender segregation and sex differences in earnings." *American Sociological Review* 52: 195-210.

TOBIN, J. (1958) "Estimation of relationships for limited dependent variables." *Econometrica* 26: 24-36.

WALTON, J., and RAGIN, C. (1990) "Global and national sources of political protest: Third World responses to the debt crisis." *American Sociological Review* 55: 876-890.

ABOUT THE AUTHOR

RICHARD BREEN is Professor of Sociology and Director of the Centre for Social Research, The Queen's University, Belfast, Northern Ireland. He has published articles on stratification, social mobility, statistical methods, and the sociology of Ireland. His most recent book is *Class Stratification: A Comparative Perspective,* coauthored with David B. Rottman.